— INSIDE —
UKRAINE

A portrait of a country and its people

by Ukraïner

BATSFORD

Introduction

Ukraïner started during my travels, when I was trying to express to people what characterized Ukraine. I found myself describing my country and hometown - or at the very least their locations - to children on the remote islands of the Indonesian archipelago, Bedouins in the Arabian desert, seniors at a Polish retirement club, tourist groups, and international festivalgoers. Over the years of travelling through various parts of the world, I realized that my conversations about Ukraine lacked the most crucial thing - an emotion. A feeling that would make a lasting impression on those I spoke with and remain forever associated in their memories with my homeland. After I returned home from my journeys around the world, I wanted to find a description of this modern-day country; a short but eloquent answer to the question 'Where are you from?'

In June 2016, a group of other like-minded people and I set off on an adventure, or, as we called it, an expedition. We announced on social media that we were going to explore Ukraine and unveil it to the world. Within a few days, we received hundreds of messages and several thousand subscribers. That's how our multimedia project Ukraïner was launched. At the very beginning of our expedition we realized how little we knew about our own country. We set off for different historical regions, learning the stories and daily lives of active and engaged citizens to highlight their valuable contributions to Ukraine, whether they were in the most remote corners of the country or in its largest cities.

At the beginning of our project we had a few dozen volunteers. Later, the Ukraïner community had a team of several hundred members that helped us create and grow every day. During the expeditions that led up to this book, everyone had their role: writers, editors and transcribers worked on the texts; directors, film editors and producers provided the video material; translators made it possible to publish our stories in several languages; there were also travellers and explorers, diplomats, media and communications experts. Together, we documented and uncovered Ukraine the way it was: real and authentic.

This book is based on over a dozen research and documentary expeditions, 100,000 kilometres on the road and more than 400 settlements that guided us through our search for the answers to the questions of 'What is Ukraine really about?' and 'Who are we?' The result is hundreds of video stories, texts and photos, many of which you can find in this book.

When Ukraïner was just at the beginning of its path, it seemed like our country had already won the war with Russia. At that time, the Ukrainians managed to stop the active offensive of the Russians and successfully distanced themselves informationally from their propaganda, leaving the deoccupation of Crimea and East of Ukraine for the future. It seemed that resilience on the information front alone would be enough for our final victory. Instead, this book was published during the full-scale Russian invasion. These pages tell stories that became not a reality of Ukraine, but its archive.

This book is only one part of the larger multimedia project available at ukrainer.net. It contains stories collected from each region, full versions of which can be found with the use of the QR codes.

Bogdan Logvynenko

Polissia

Volyn

Halychyna

The Carpathians

Zakarpattia

Bukovyna

Podillia

Naddnipr

Prychorno

Bessarabia

A Note from the British Publisher

This book came into my hands as a gift from the Ukrainian family I was hosting in London. It, along with the mother and two girls, had travelled 30 hours to get to us, via a bus, a train journey to the Polish border and then a flight from Krakow. They didn't know I was a book publisher and my immediate interest was a surprise to them. It was obvious both that they needed to sleep, and that the book needed to be published in the English-speaking world. It was written before the war and it is a wonderful portrait of what it means to be Ukrainian. Thank you for buying this book.

Polly Powell, Batsford

Contents

Zakarpattia

Michel and his Buffaloes

Ecologist Michel Jacobi came to Ukraine from Germany to conserve Ukraine's ecosystem and traditional stock-breeding practices.

Despite the fact that modern animal husbandry norms favour cows and intensive farming practices, Michel began to breed buffaloes. In the early 20th century, raising buffalo was common in Zakarpattia; there were several thousand buffaloes in the neighbouring villages. When the communists came to power, all the buffaloes were placed in collective farms. But the female buffaloes did not take to their new conditions and stopped producing milk. By the 1990s, the buffalo population had declined from a few thousand to around one hundred.

'I thought that in Ukraine I could find the same natural environment and lifestyle of our ancestors since they don't exist in Germany anymore. People need to live in harmony with nature. I want to show this by my own example.'

With the support of a few charity foundations and village leaders who gave him some land that previously belonged to the collective farms, Michel began assembling his buffalo herd from the surrounding areas.

Michel watches over his herd at farms in Chumaliovo and Steblivka and works on a breed registry. Michel also has buffaloes living along the semi-wild shores of the Danube.

Traian Mustiatse

Mount Yavirnyk, Yanko Derevlianyi

Artist, sculptor and architect Yanko Derevlianyi, looking for a place to live in harmony with nature, chose Yavirnyk, a mountain near the town of Velykyi Bereznyi, to set up his workshop. Yanko first came to Yavirnyk in 1974 when he was working as an interior designer at a Soviet-era tourist complex. Since then he has been very active in the area designing and building huts and fire-pits for travellers.

'Even cats run wild on the mountain, and it's a rare soul that can spend much time here.'

Taras Kovalchuk   13

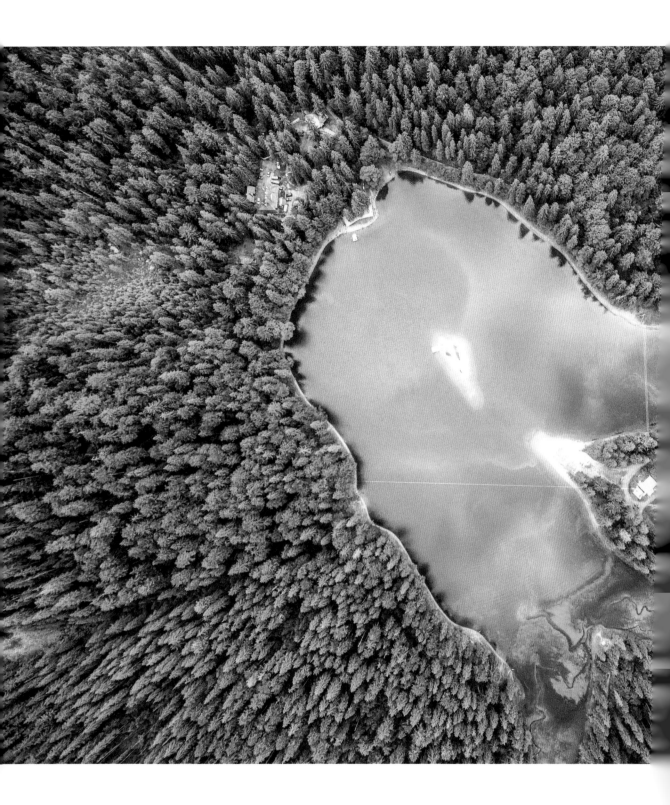

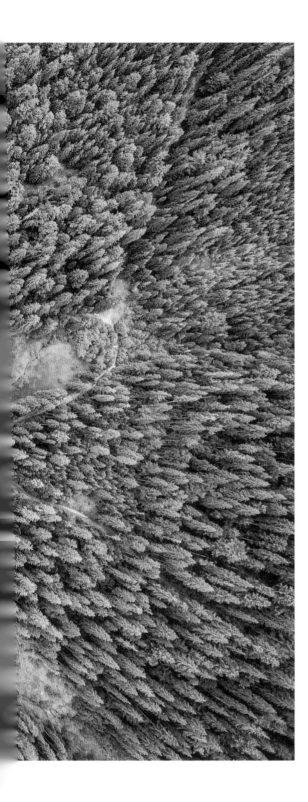

Synevyr is the largest mountain lake in Ukraine, located at 989 metres above sea level in the Vnutrishni (Inner) Gorgany mountain range in the Carpathians.

The Borzhava Narrow-gauge Railway

Locals call the Borzhava narrow-gauge railway, built at the beginning of the 20th century, 'Antsia'. The train is drawn by an old diesel locomotive TU-2, produced in the 1950s. Vynohradiv train station is one of the favourite meeting points for the locals and it also hosts a market.

Antsia is only one of a few active narrow-gauge railways in Ukraine, with a rail width of 750 millimetres. Its route, from Vynohradiv through Khmilnyk to Irshava, is 123 kilometres long. The main rail goes along the Borzhava River, from which the name of the railway is derived. The two carriages and the old locomotive cross the market in Vynohradiv carrying the passengers through Zakarpattia.

In the 1930s, the village of Kolochava was mentioned in the novel *Nikola the Outlaw*, by Czech author Ivan Olbracht, who had lived there for several years. The book made Kolochava village a popular destination for Czech tourists. Nowadays, Kolochava is home to many museums and an unforgettably picturesque road along the river leading to the village.

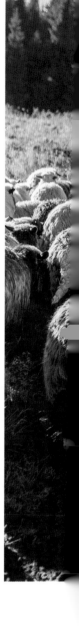

The Vlachs

Vlachs are an ethnic group found all over Central and South-east Europe. The majority of the Vlachs in Ukraine live in villages throughout Zakarpattia and Bessarabia. Living in relatively closed communities, they are primarily woodworkers and shepherds. One of their shepherds' huts is near Mount Pidpula, part of the Svydovets massif in the Carpathians. For a few months every year, the Vlachs graze their flocks here and cook traditional meals using fresh ingredients provided by their sheep.

Carolling in Dovhe

Traditional koliada-singing (carolling) is performed on the 7 and 8 January in Dovhe, Zakarpattia.

Older boys dress up as shepherds and one is given the role of an old man. The youngest boys, dressed as angels, have the hardest mission: carrying the wooden 'vertep' (portable puppet theatre) called a 'betlehem' in the local dialect. It is very heavy, and with each house the children pass they become increasingly tired. The boys are supposed to alternate who carries the vertep every five houses, but they often lose count.

The older boys don't have it easy, either. The costumes are uncomfortable, the text is easy to forget, and they need to make it through the younger children's constant arguing. But they are at least treated to some homemade alcohol after they carol at a house. As the 'responsible one', the 'old man' can't drink. The 'shepherds', on the other hand, don't mind indulging themselves from time to time!

The Roma of Korolevo

One-third of the Roma in Ukraine live in densely populated settlements in Zakarpattia. Ukraine is home to some 40,000 Roma, according to data from NGOs working with the Roma population. The compact Roma settlements in Zakarpattia are designed as residential areas with separate streets, quarters or neighbourhoods.

The population of the Korolevo settlement in the Vynohradiv district is home to over 3,700 people. This is one of the best-planned Roma settlements in Zakarpattia. The houses here are made of bricks and sometimes even have more than one storey. The roads are gravelled, children run happily around on the streets, and the girls wear traditional Roma dresses.

Clothing is a very important status symbol for the women. Skirts are embroidered with gold and silver, and clothes are decorated with glass jewellery. Family jewellery is often

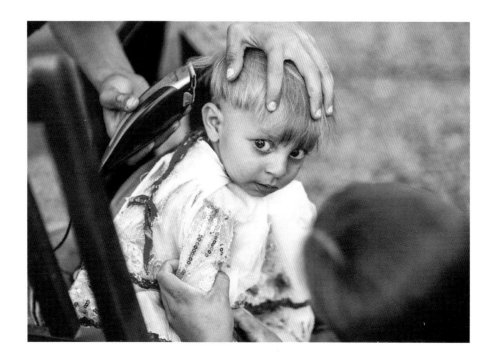

very valuable and usually custom-made. These family jewels will serve as the a dowry for a bride, a symbol of her family's prosperity.

Men from Korolevo work in teams consisting of close relatives and neighbours. Together they make the parts for tin roofs and rain gutters. Craftsmen here have a long-established reputation and their own style of decoration.

Pryazovia

A dried-up football field in the village of Hryhorivka.

Askania-Nova

Askania-Nova is the biggest steppe biosphere reserve in Europe and the oldest in the world. It has featured on the list of the UNESCO World Network of Biosphere Reserves since 1984.

In 1898, a German, Friedrich-Jacob Eduardovych Falz-Fein, gave the first 600 hectares of land to the reserve. As a researcher, he wanted to observe how nature would develop without human interference. He had been spending a significant part of his income on development of a zoo and preservation of the steppe reserve.

Viktor Havrylenko, the managing director of Askania-Nova, knows every square metre of this land. His car alone is allowed to enter the reserve as it is the only one the wild animals are used to.

'I tell my colleagues that I am the wildest among them. Nobody has lived in the forest, away from any kind of human settlement, longer than I have.'

Nowadays, Askania-Nova's ecosystem includes more than 500 plant species and over 3,000 animal species. Here, you can study the behaviour of zebras, bison and antelopes in a semi-wild environment very similar to their natural habitats.

Berdiansk

The Soviet-era railway tracks running right along the waterfront at Berdiansk have become an iconic image of the town.

Botieve and the Bulgarians

Pryazovia is a multicultural region. Bulgarians, Greeks, Albanians, Germans and many other nationalities have co-existed here for centuries.

The ethnic Bulgarian community in Pryazovia emerged after a wave of immigration that lasted from 1861 to 1862. Coming from Bessarabia, these Bulgarian settlers founded more than 30 villages.

During the 1990s, many societies of Bulgarian culture have been established. As a result of their efforts, folk bands were formed and the Bulgarian language was introduced both at schools and in newspapers.

We see hope for the future of the Bulgarian language and traditions in Pryazovia precisely because the Bulgarian culture preserved here has such a unique and distinctive character.

The Slag Heaps of Mariupol

Mariupol, a city of factories and the sea, is located in the south-east of Ukraine. About 100,000 people out of the city's half a million work at local factories.

Huge slag heaps of waste material from heavy industry have become the landmarks of the city. Huge hills of draw rocks are usually located near factories.

During the early stages of the Russian-Ukrainian conflict, there was a time when Mariupol was under occupation. Immediately after the Ukrainian government took back control, Mariupol began investing in new infrastructure projects, from new co-working spaces and playgrounds, to concert and theatre halls. This will help to prepare the city for the eventual closure of the factories by developing new sectors and broadening the labour market. Hopefully, the strategy will cushion against possible economic decline and give the city a new focus.

The Molokans of Novovasylivka

The religious community of the Molokans is a branch of Spiritual Christianity, though the traditional church regards them as a sect. These Christians spread to Pryazovia from Russia in the 18th century. Molokans were fleeing the Empire to reach its borderlands in order to preserve their religion based on old rituals.

Molokans differ from members of the Russian Orthodox church: they don't have icons, they drink milk during Lent and they don't accept the sacrament. Their religious traditions are very simple: they sing spiritual songs and listen to sermons during their prayer meetings.

People know very little about Molokans, but the village of Novovasylivka in Pryazovia is the most famous centre for this fellowship of Old Believers.

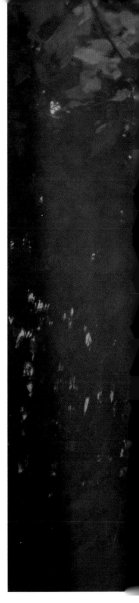

Photographer Oleksandr Prykhnenko

Oleksandr Prykhnenko is a shipbuilder, writer and photographer from the town of Henichesk. Oleksandr has accomplished much in his 80 years: he has visited several dozen countries, published 26 books and made a documentary.

Serhiy Korovayny

Kamiana Mohyla

Kamiana Mohyla is a unique rock formation in the middle of the Pryazovia steppe. From above, this hill of boulders resembles the human brain. Long ago, people believed that unusual natural landmarks like these were endowed with mystical properties, and would treat them as outdoor shrines.

Rock carvings from different periods can be found in the grottos and caves of Kamiana Mohyla. The carvings have lost their definition over time since they were cut into the soft surface of sandstone. Today the place is shrouded in legend.

Poltavshchyna

Carpet Production in Reshetylivka

The town of Reshetylivka is one of the historical centres of carpet manufacturing in Ukraine. It has been known for its master artisans since the 19th century. Reshetylivka developed as a centre of arts and crafts due to the high-quality fine wool from a local breed of sheep and its unique embroidery and weaving techniques. Even though mechanization and commercialization are steadily superseding the local businesses and traditional methods, there are still several carpet producers in Reshetylivka.

In the Soviet times, artists from all over the USSR would come to Reshetylivka, just as Yevhen and Larysa Piliuhin did. The talented couple were offered a job at the local college as folk art specialists. The Piliuhins continue to develop the art and industry of carpet-making and work to ensure that their skills are passed onto the next generation.

Horishni Plavni, Vasyl Leshchenko - the Yachtsman

Horishni Plavni is an industrial town on the banks of the Kamianske Reservoir. Several villages were demolished for the construction of the mineral processing plant. The town is named after the wetlands, called 'plavni' in Ukrainian, that encircle the town. The water recreation area led to the development of amateur yachting as a popular pastime and even a shipbuilding yard. Back in the 1970s, a yacht club was founded in Horishni Plavni.

Vasyl Leshchenko has built about ten yachts in his garage. His yacht *Frigate* is now one of the town's symbols. Vasyl's interest in shipbuilding began with model wooden boats.

'In 1972, I bought a simple wooden boat for 10 rubles and used ordinary bedsheets for the sails. We used to sail on this little boat with my family whenever we went swimming.'

Taras Kovalchuk   51

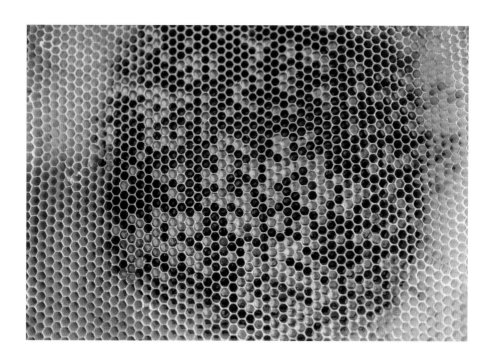

Yuryivka, Ivan Hura - the Beekeeper

Yuryivka is so small that no one has bothered to give it a signpost. What was once a populous village, with over 60 households and about 300 residents, is now home to fewer than 20 people. Despite this, Yuryivka boasts the largest apiary in the region, with over 100 beehives. Ivan Hura manages the whole production.

If it were not for the apiary, it is likely that the village would no longer exist.

'Once, at an alumni reunion, my former classmates asked, "Who is that idiot who settled down in Yuryivka?" I replied proudly, "I am!"'

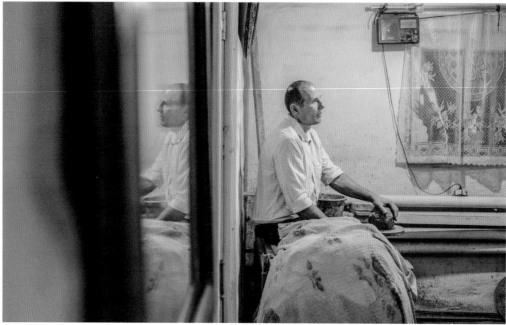

The Potters of Opishne

There are about ten pottery centres in Ukraine and Opishne in Poltavshchyna is the largest. The area is rich in clay deposits. From the end of the 19th century to the beginning of the 20th century, one out of three families here worked in the industry.

The great variety of shapes and sizes in ceramics emerged to complement the needs of Ukraine's many culinary dishes and diverse cultural traditions.

Opishne's traditional pottery painting is characterized by floral motifs such as flowers, grapes, wheat ears and branches. Warm red and brown hues are accented by touches of green and blue.

Serhiy Korovayny 55

Panasivka, Valerii Yermakov

Panasivka is a village located on the left bank of the Psel River in Poltavshchyna near Myrhorod. Finding Panasivka on the map requires some effort and there is no public transport to the town. There are just 20 people now living in the village. Those that do find their way there will see the flags of Greece and Ukraine fluttering next to the sign for Panasivka. It indicates that this place is the home of Valerii Yermakov, a sculptor and artist.

Prior to Ukraïner's expedition visit, Valerii was virtually unknown. However, he admits that fame was never something he wanted to pursue. Valerii has been living a solitary life since his wife died a few years ago. At the age of 79, Valerii is one of the youngest men in the village. He has turned his yard into an open-air gallery for his distinctive sculptures.

Valerii admires Nikolai Gogol (whose famous story *The Fair at Sorochyntsi* is set within 10 kilometres of here) and Greek mythology. With no formal art education or life models, he uses only magazines as a guide.

'People strive for material wealth. I, on the other hand, only want to be able to create, and to have enough strength and courage.'

After meeting Valerii, we came up with the idea of arranging a trip to Greece for him and making a film about it. The Ukraïner team applied to several companies to support this project, but to no avail. We decided to raise the necessary funds to realize Valerii's dream by launching a fundraising campaign on Facebook. Almost 850 people donated a total of around $4,000 USD and helped Valerii's dream of visiting the home of Greek mythology come true.

Serhiy Korovayny   59

Pavlo Pashko, Mykola Nosok

A Journey from Panasivka to Greece

In March 2018, sculptor Valerii Yermakov travelled abroad for the first time in his life. His journey through Greece, a country that had inspired him since childhood, lasted for 11 days. His specially planned itinerary focused on exploring Athens, Delphi and the Peloponnese peninsula.

Following his return to Ukraine, Valerii held his very first press conference. He spoke about the Ukrainian and Greek people he had met on his trip, among which were the mayors of Olympia and Zacharo. He described the museums he had visited and reflected on his experience in Greece, a country he had once only dreamed about from books and films. At home in Panasivka, Valerii made a private display for his fellow villagers; Valerii placed a Greek flag near the Ukrainian one, next to the road sign for Panasivka.

Kriachkivka, Jurij Fedynskyj

Jurij Fedynskyj was born into a family of Ukrainian immigrants in the USA. At the age of 23, Jurij moved to Ukraine, but views it as coming home rather than moving.

As a child, Jurij came across a pre-war recording of bandura players in his family's collection. The melodies and the voice touched him. After this introduction to Ukrainian culture, he became interested in the art of the kobzars (wandering folk bards), Ukrainian music and folk instruments. Jurij received a degree in music in Detroit and after that travelled across the USA performing Ukrainian music.

He later continued his studies in Ukraine and received his second degree.

'It is safe to say that I came back home 250 years after the destruction of the Zaporizhian Cossack Sich.'

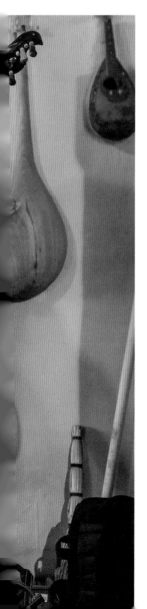

Jurij Fedynskyj and his wife Maria have built a workshop for musical instruments in Kriachkivka. Much was lost during the Soviet era in terms of traditional musical instrument-making, sound and playing. Jurij and Maria work to restore what was lost. Their newly built village house has a studio with several dozen traditional instruments – kobzas, banduras, torbans, lyres and husli (an instrument belonging to the zither family).

Polissia

The Singing of Polissia

Polissia is famous for its authentic singing techniques with a great number of changes in range. The singing is an integral part of work, leisure, traditional ceremonies and rites.

There is neither a village hall nor a shop in Svalovychi village, and a truck delivers bread there just once a week. Kateryna Trush lives here alone in her house – her husband died a long time ago and her children have moved out.

'You can walk through Svalovychi, and you won't find anyone who can sing for you the way I do! They send everyone to me because nobody can sing old songs the way I can.'

If you ask Kateryna how many songs she knows, she answers with a smile, 'A hundred thousand and one!'

The singing usually involves two to three voices. Although the number of villagers is decreasing, there are still some locals here who remember and preserve the songs. The singing of Polissia attracts both Ukrainians and visitors from other countries who want to learn this unique art.

Wild Honey Farmers in Kniazivka

Wild honey farming ('bortnytstvo') is an old practice of harvesting honey from wild bees. Many sources considered this tradition to have been lost in Ukraine after the 18th and 19th centuries. However, wild honey hunters still exist in Polissia.

The name of this craft originates from wooden logs where bees live - 'borts'. Hollow logs, cut with an axe, are hung on trees as high up as possible. This positioning contributes to the unique taste of honey, gathered from when the trees first blossom in spring to the late flowers of autumn.

Yurii and Tetiana Starynski from the village of Kniazivka learned the art of bortnytstvo from their parents. They wish their children also followed their family business - they are the last wild honey farmers in this village.

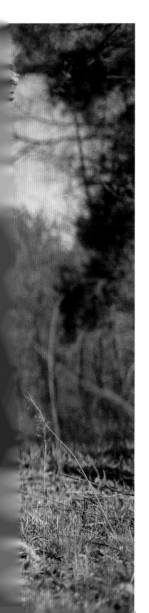

'This activity calms me down. Anything can happen in this life due to stress. When I feel stressed, I just go to my bees, stand next to their beehive, and let everything go just watching them.'

Serhiy Korovayny   69

The Antonivka-Zarichne Narrow-gauge Railway

The Antonivka-Zarichne narrow-gauge railway has been operating for over 115 years. The locals call it Polissia tram or 'Kukushka' ('cuckoo'). For some villages along the route, it is the only transport available. Along the way, the train crosses the wooden and metal bridge over the Styr River.

This bridge is unique in Ukraine. The track starts from the town of Antonivka and stretches 106 kilometres to Zarichne. This is the longest narrow-gauge railway in Europe.

Grazing cows at pasture near Mlynok village.

The Self-settlers of Chornobyl

On the night of 26 April 1986, the disaster at the Chornobyl Nuclear Power Plant took place. Only after several days did authorities inform the population about the scale of the catastrophe and begin evacuation. People were forcibly relocated from the territories now known as the Exclusion Zone.

When the level of contamination in the area was officially announced, the majority of evacuated people were scared to return to their homes, and almost everyone stayed away. Everyone but the self-settlers.

Most of these people, driven by homesickness, returned during the first year after the accident. Even barbed wire and the army could not stop them. Some did not leave the area at all. They hid from the soldiers in barns or cellars and ignored evacuation notices. Also, those who worked at the Chornobyl Nuclear Power Plant and its subsidiaries

remained in the Zone by default: they were given temporary passes that were renewed annually.

The villagers of the Chornobyl Exclusion Zone call themselves 'self-settlers'; they are being ironic though, as the place is actually their home.

Oleksandr Khomenko

The Chornobyl Exclusion Zone

The Exclusion Zone emerged after the Chornobyl Nuclear Power Plant disaster. At first, it was a totally restricted area, even for those who lived there. Nowadays, it is a popular tourist destination.

The town of Prypiat, located just 2 kilometres away from the plant, is a monument to human neglect. It is abandoned and contaminated by radiation. In the absence of human activity, the forest took over the area.

It is now inhabited by wild animals and their population is constantly growing. At the same time, it is a town-museum of international importance, a monument to this enormous technological catastrophe.

Another popular destination nearby is the Duha radar complex ('duha' means 'arch'), built in the 1970s as a large-scale air defence project, part of the Cold War arms race. This secret complex cost the USSR almost twice as much as

the construction of the Chornobyl Nuclear Power Plant, but was never put into regular operation. After the Chornobyl disaster, Duha was decommissioned, and has since become a site of interest for tourists.

Pavlo Pashko, Oleksandr Khomenko

The Hoich Hamlet

The hamlet of Zelenyi Hai is located 120 kilometres from Kyiv. The old-timers call it Hoich, which means 'forest clearing' in the local dialect. The hamlet has only 11 houses. A journalist from Kyiv, Kateryna Mizina, has bought one of them. Gradually she has turned this place into an art space. Together with friends, she organizes festivals, movie screenings and art projects.

'People often have no space to get to know each other, to talk, to work, to dig the soil, to polish wood and so on. Occupational therapy can be a wonderful thing indeed. The air is excellent here as well as the conditions: there is neither the Internet nor a good phone signal here. This brings people together – they unplug and start communicating.'

Mykola and Tetiana Vaskevych from the village of Komory hold a photo of themselves when they were young. The couple are preserving the local tradition of singing. Previously, everyone used to sing in Komory, but nowadays less than 40 residents remain and most of them are in their seventies or older.

The Quarries of Korostyshiv

Korostyshiv is famous for the extraction and processing of granite on a huge scale. Nowadays, hundreds of small entrepreneurs use the site of the former Soviet enterprise to produce large granite blocks. The deposits of granite in the area are still impressive. The old quarries, though, have become tourist attractions. Former deposit extraction sites have been filled with water.

The most popular flooded quarry is shaped like a horseshoe and has a deep lake in the middle. Its rocky banks are covered with pines, firs and birches. The cliffs that overhang the water have somewhere climbers come to train.

Oleksandr Ratushnyak   83

Bessarabia

Pelicans

In summer, 70 per cent of the world's great white pelicans (*Pelecanus onocrotalus*) reside in the Danube Delta, between the territories of Ukraine and Romania.

Sheep Breeders

Sheep breeding is quite common in the steppe areas of
Southern Ukraine and in the mountainous areas of the
Carpathians. In Bessarabian villages, local ethnic groups
of Bulgarians, Gagauz and Moldovans are usually involved
in sheep breeding. Traditions often differ between the
villages, which are scattered all over the region.

Serhiy Korovayny, Oleksandr Ratushnyak   89

Vylkove, the Town on the Water

Vylkove is a unique Ukrainian town located in the Danube estuary where the river enters the Black Sea. For a long time, local people have been moving around through the channels known as 'yeryks'. Sadly, yeryks are being filled in and turned into roads for vehicles. On the yeryks that still exist, people use motor boats or traditional boats, which they sail standing up using a single oar. There are also wooden jetties for pedestrians along the banks of the canals.

Frumushyka-Nova

Frumushyka-Nova is a contemporary reconstruction of the village that was founded here in the 18th century, which was completely demolished to make way for an army training facility during the Soviet era. In 2006, the Palariiev family began to restore the village based on mapping records. They established a museum and recreation complex, as well as one of the largest sheep farms in Europe. The world's tallest statue of a shepherd was also erected here.

The 16.4-metre monument has already been registered in the Guinness World Records.

'This monument costs as much as a kilometre of road pavement. We need 18 kilometres of road to be paved. Doesn't it make sense to create an object worth paving a road to?'

Tourists come to Frumushyka-Nova to take a look at another of Ukraine's unique places – the open-air museum of socialist realism. In the middle of the steppe, there are over a hundred sculptures depicting leaders and significant figures from Soviet times. Lenin, Brezhnev, Stalin, Chkalov, Kirov and Chapayev greet sunrises and watch the sunsets that are just incredible in this area.

Serhiy Korovayny, Pavlo Pashko   93

The Tuzly Estuaries

The Tuzly Estuaries National Nature Park is a chain of 13 estuaries at the confluence of the rivers Danube and Dnister. The core of the park comprises the salty estuaries of Shahany, Alibey, Burnas and some other smaller lagoons. The estuaries are separated from the Black Sea by a 36-kilometre spit of land.

The territory of the park includes the full variety of local flora and fauna - you can see more than 300 species of birds and 40 types of animals, while the waters contain around 60 kinds of fish.

Pavlo Pashko

Lacarin - the Winemaker from Shabo

Christophe Lacarin de Fabiani is a French entrepreneur, perfumer and winemaker. He grows 14 varieties of grape on the shore of the Dnister Estuary. In 2016, he received an official licence to produce wine commercially. He produces his wine by hand and uses no chemical ingredients. His love of animals encouraged him to stock his land with goats, chickens, horses and sheep. In Shabo, Monsieur Lacarin has found a perfect place for both work and life - with great soil, a mild climate and fresh air.

'Life isn't just about work, is it? One cannot think about money all the time. Be happy. Enjoy life.'

Zatoka

Zatoka is a popular resort in the Odesa region.

Its southern side is located on the Budzhak spit that separates the Black Sea and the Budzhak estuary. The rest of the settlement is situated on the Karolino-Buhaz spit between the Black Sea and the Dnister Estuary.

Following the annexation of Crimea by Russia, Zatoka beach has attracted increasing numbers of tourists.

Serhiivka, the Yachting School

Serhiivka is a resort town not far from Odesa that has become a centre for yachting. It is located on the shore of the Budzhak estuary. Students at the yachting school founded by Viacheslav and Oleksandr Smetanka practise here. The first international competitions took place in Serhiivka in the 1990s. Viacheslav Smetanka also dreams of organizing yachting courses for children from other parts of Ukraine.

'We have everything here: hot water, therapeutic mud, a lot of fish and pelicans that have chosen Ukraine as their native land and always come back to us. We want our children to grow and live here, not leave for somewhere else.'

Utkonosivka, the Valley of Tomatoes

The tomato-growing centre of Bessarabia is in the village of Utkonosivka. It has 4,000 residents, and the majority of them grow vegetables, mainly tomatoes. The village is known for particular variety of tomato called 'Primadonna'. This tomato is recognizable by its distinctive, pointed tip or 'nose'. Another unique feature of the village is that each property has a greenhouse.

Until 1947, the village was called Ördek-Burnu, which means 'duck's beak' in the Nogai language. If you look at a map you will see that the outline of the village resembles a duck. The modern name of the village - Utkonosivka (literally 'duck's nose') - is derived from wordplay and a pun from translation. The village is located near Katlabukh Lake; it is 16 kilometres from the Danube and 50 kilometres from the Black Sea and the Danube Delta Biosphere Reserve.

Pavlo Pashko, Oleksandr Ratushnyak   103

The Buffaloes of Orlivka

The village of Orlivka is surrounded by water. The Danube reed beds surround it on one side, and there are a number of large lakes on the other. The straits become overgrown with reeds and filled with silt, and the land gets flooded. Black buffaloes help to save the local ecosystem.

Ecologist Michel Jacobi brought one of his herds here from Zakarpattia. The buffaloes are well-adjusted to changes in climate; they graze plants in the water, helping to clear the channels.

This solar power station near the village of Starokozache covers 80 hectares.

Sivershchyna

Snovsk, the Tkachenko Brothers

Oleh and Viktor Tkachenko are twin brothers working as mechanics in the locomotive depot in the town of Snovsk. Their depot is one of the only few remaining in Ukraine that carries out specialized repair of steam locomotives.

Oleh and Viktor, together with their younger brother Mykhailo, are members of a small team of mechanics who still have the skills to repair unique models of steam trains, the majority of which date from the end of the 19th century.

Ferries on the Desna River

The Desna is one of the largest rivers in Ukraine. There are many settlements along its banks, but nowadays very few ferries that connect them are operating. There are ferries in the villages of Desnianske, Radychiv and Mezyn villages, and down the river in Sosnytsia and Makoshyne. Also, there are pontoon crossings at Byryne and Maksaky.

Ferries are still used daily to get to towns, markets and elsewhere more quickly than via roads and bridges.

Even if there is only one person needing to cross the river, a ferryman will not refuse to take them.

'Well, I'm not as global as the state. The state can neglect couple of hundred of people, but for me, even if there is only one person, I will provide transport.'

The ferry operates daily until the Desna freezes in winter. When this happens a special crossing is created for cars to drive over the ice.

Obyrok

The hamlet of Obyrok is an artistic settlement near the town of Bakhmach. It was created by merging several smaller hamlets: Katsiry, Prokhory and Koroli. This place, surrounded by pine woods, is ideal for relaxation and art events.

Among the most noteworthy art objects at Obyrok are several Soviet-era monuments with trees growing over them. In this 'Garden of the Empire Decay', nature unmercifully destroys what used to be considered indestructible.

The hamlet was founded by film director Leonid Kanter, who travelled around the world in 2010 to place kitchen stools on the shores of four oceans: in France, Sri Lanka, Spitsbergen and Cape Horn. During this trip, Leonid shot the documentary that became the basis for the film *Human with a Stool*.

The Mezyn National Nature Park covers over 31,000 hectares. More than 50 archaeological features are preserved here. The most famous is a Mezyn Palaeolithic site. There are a number of historical settlements around the park and nearby; these include buildings, temples and park complexes.

Oleshnia, the Potter Ivan Bibik

The village of Oleshnia has long been famous for its potters.

'In our village, a girl wouldn't go out with a guy if he didn't have a potter's wheel.'

These are the words of Ivan Bibik, one of the last potters in Oleshnia. Today, there are just a few of them in the entire village. Ivan's family has been making pottery for generations. Like many other potters in Oleshnia, he learned the craft when he was still a child. Ivan earned his first money for the small plates he made and sold at the market together with his father's handiwork. Visitors from all over Ukraine come to learn pottery skills from Ivan, though his own children have chosen not to continue the family business.

Mykyta Zavilinskyi   119

Kachanivka is the largest country estate in Ukraine in the neoclassical style. It was built in the 1770s as the residence of Count Rumyantsev-Zadunaisky.

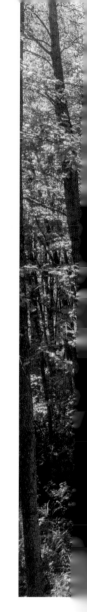

Mizhrichynskyi Park

Mizhrichynskyi Park is among the largest regional landscape parks in Ukraine, and covers 100,000 hectares. The territory between the Dnipro and the Desna rivers ('mizhrichchia' in Ukrainian, from which the name of the park is derived) is one of the southernmost taiga landscapes.

There are moss swamps, moorlands, sand dunes and glades with sparse trees in the park. At its centre is a forest that provides a refuge for wildlife. The lynx, which can be found here, forms part of the emblem of the park.

Yurii Dakhno's Museum in Moskali

In the village of Moskali, near Chernihiv, less than 20 houses remain. The main street, 1 kilometre in length, has neither a school nor a medical centre. However, there is a museum.

A local resident, Yurii Dakhno, created his own Skansen here: he bought some of the old houses and a shop and turned them into museums. The exhibits include household items from the 19th and 20th centuries, together with artwork from local artists. In the former shop there are paintings on the walls and glass bottles and mugs on the shelves, wooden barrels, straw hats hanging on pegs, a gramophone, an old radio and shoes hidden behind the drawers.

The houses contain more furniture: chests, wooden beds and chairs that are typical of rural life in the 1940s and 1950s.

Yurii bought most of the items from local people, but some exhibits come from craftsmen outside the area. He says he knows the origin of almost all of the pieces.

The museum was not created for profit - visitors are rare here, but sometimes guests from other parts of Ukraine or foreigners stop by. Yurii says that his collection is his creative escape.

The display Yurii has gathered is valuable for ethnography. In 1932, most of the village burned down, so the clothes and tools that survived have become a rarity.

The Blakytni ('Blue') Lakes near the village of Oleshnia in Sivershchyna are quarries that have been filled by natural springs and are surrounded by pine woods. Quartz sand used in glass production was previously extracted here. The biggest of the four lakes is called Velyke ('Big'); some people also call it Sertse ('Heart') because of its shape.

Pavlo Pashko   127

Podillia

Zalishchyky

Zalishchyky is situated on a peninsula surrounded by the Dnister River. Due to its unique location, the town borders three regions – Podillia, Bukovyna and Halychyna. Since a railway was built in the 19th century, this place began to attract increasing numbers of tourists. The resort became popular due to its climate, which is similar to the Mediterranean. The steep slopes of the Dnister valley around the peninsula do not allow the warm air to escape. To get to Zalishchyky, you need to use either one of the two bridges or take a ferry from the other bank of the Dnister River.

The Broom Republic

The villages of Savran, Osychky and Vilshanka are best known for their tradition of broom-making. People call them 'environmentally friendly vacuum cleaners'. Children, teenagers, adults and elderly people alike are involved with broom weaving. For an experienced craftsperson, it takes only five minutes to finish one broom. However, it all depends on the person, their personality and how quickly they work.

To local people, broom weaving means additional income. It is a family tradition that has been passed from generation to generation. People make brooms during the week, and then sell them at the market in Savran, which opens at 7am on Thursdays. There is less than an hour to buy everything on the list. The market is not open for long and brooms can only be bought wholesale; they come in packs, with 50 brooms in each.

Bakota

Bakota, a flooded village not far from Kamianets-Podilskyi, is known for its picturesque landscapes. In 1981, due to the construction of Novodnistrovsk Hydropower Plant, all local residents were forced to move to the nearest towns. Bakota and other villages nearby were flooded. Nowadays, this reservoir is 200 kilometres long, and the flooded fields cover an area of 1,590 hectares.

Bakota was founded as a town and was mentioned for the first time in a chronicle from 1240 as the largest administrative centre of Dnister Ponyzzia, with over 3,000 inhabitants. In the 13-14th centuries, the area between the Dnister and the Buh rivers was known as Rus Dolna, with its capital in Bakota. It used to be a crossing point for both land and water trade routes.

Oleksii Karpovych 135

Motoball

Motoball is a type of sport played exclusively in Europe. It originally came from France and became popular in Ukraine during the Soviet period. In Kamianets-Podilskyi, motoball dates back to 1966. A stadium designed specifically for it was built in 1982.

A motoball field resembles a football pitch in terms of dimensions, but the markings are slightly different: there is no circle in the centre, and the goalposts are in the shape of a semi-circle. The surface is normally covered with asphalt or gravel. To allow for the manoeuvring capabilities of motorcycles, the asphalt needs to be dusted with sand. The ball used is several times larger than a standard football. A team consists of five players, including a goalkeeper, each riding a motorbike.

In Ukraine, a game lasts for four periods of 15 minutes each. In other European countries, game has three periods of 20 minutes each. For a single game, each motorcycle requires 5 litres of fuel; the same is needed for training.

Polina Zabizhko

Malanka Celebrations in Osychky

The folk holiday of Malanka takes place on 13 January and the celebrations in the village of Osychky are absolutely authentic, as the people have managed to preserve their old traditions without interference from tourists or the media.

The main characters include Malanka, who is played by a boy, aged between four and seven years old, dressed as a girl; a Cossack, wearing a military uniform from the Soviet era, who accompanies Malanka on her way to each house; singers performing traditional carols ('koliadkas') outside every house; and Didoks, mystical figures who behave in a wild and shocking manner whose main task is to protect Malanka.

Hot Air Balloons

The long-established city of Kamianets-Podilskyi is known for its fortress, its eclectic mix of cultures from various nations and its vibrant festival life. The most remarkable of these is the hot air balloon festival.

Its proponents believe that Kamianets-Podilskyi has every chance of becoming an aeronautics centre. It was the suitability of the terrain for different manoeuvres that encouraged people there to found an aeronautics club.

Twice a year, the city hosts hot air balloon festivals. At the beginning of May, the season starts with the Podillia Cup festival, followed by the Golden Omega festival in October.

'It's like yachting. Although yachts only use one horizontal plane, while we have got an endless number of different planes.'

Bukatynka, the Alioshkin Museum

Bukatynka is famous for its unique landscapes - remnants of rock layers from previous geological eras. It is also the site of ancient volcanic eruptions, ancient oceans and deserts. This village used to be a centre for the craft of stone cutting. Maintaining traditions and collecting examples of this ancient craft were the main reasons why artists Oleksii and Liudmyla Alioshkin settled in Bukatynka more than 40 years ago. They founded a gallery that exhibits various sculptures, each conveying a unique message. At first, the couple lived in a dug-out hut. Then, with their parents' help, they built a two-storey house. When abandoned houses in the neighbourhood came up for sale, the Alioshkins bought them and turned them into museums.

The Fortress of Kamianets-Podilskyi

The fortress of Kamianets-Podilskyi is among the most renowned fortifications in Ukraine. It towers above the rocky headland while the surrounding cliffs of the Smotrych River serve as natural barriers. While the first fortifications were built during the times of the Kyivan Rus between the 9th and 13th centuries, it was not until the 15–17th centuries that the fortress began to resemble the site we see today. The indomitable spirit of the medieval outpost leaves a strong impression. Now it is an open-air museum featuring copies of traditional crafts from various historical periods.

From Odesa to Shershentsi

The village of Shershentsi is located in the valley of the River Biloch, on the border with Moldova. Before Dmytro Skoryk and his wife Nadia moved there, they had lived in Odesa for 35 years. Within a few years, they renovated a traditional manor house in the village, set up their own brand, and launched their business. The couple host tourists in the Bilochi manor house, where they can enjoy home-made cooking.

The Skoryk family decided to revive their ancestors' traditions. They want to prove it themselves and everyone else that it is possible to live off the land without relying on someone else's money. Dmytro and Nadia know, preserve and try to create Ukrainian traditions. It all started on their wedding day, when they dressed in the traditional Ukrainian dress, specific to this region.

'After our wedding in 2008, people in the neighbourhood started to value traditions and incorporate them into their everyday lives. Our traditions are something to be proud of. They are priceless.'

An unusual aerial view of crop fields.

The Carpathians

The Buddhists of Donetsk

One of the oldest Buddhist communities in Ukraine, originating from Donetsk, is located near the village of Kryvopillia. The monks shave their heads and wear white gowns with orange cloaks. They wake up at dawn to read prayers to the sun. Their appearance and lifestyle are unconventional compared to most Ukrainians, but the monks live in the Carpathians and speak Ukrainian.

The first Buddhist religious community was officially registered in Donetsk in 1991. Before the war with Russia broke out, the activity of Buddhist centres in independent Ukraine had been mostly focused in the Slobozhanshchyna region.

Serhii Filonenko, a monk of the Lotus Sutra Order, told us that their community was founded just after Ukraine proclaimed its independence, and was registered with the help of Ukrainian theologist Ihor Kozlovskyi.

Green Construction in Slavske

Architects Eduard Pastukh and Olha Sukha are involved in green construction in the Carpathians. They design energy-efficient homes and are constantly looking for natural, sustainable building materials. The most popular of these are straw, hemp, petroleum and clay.

'Ecology is all about optimized spaces you live in. It is the ability to appreciate the important and to get rid of the unnecessary. It is understanding what you really need.'

The social aspect of this green project is very important to the couple. In the village of Slavske, they have founded a platform for creative experiences and retreats – Creative Residence MC-6. People come here to see the viability of green technologies and to get a real feel for green materials.

Dmytro Bartosh 155

The Ornithopter

An amateur inventor, Volodymyr Yakovenko has been living in the village of Iltsi for more than 30 years. He researches, designs, builds and tests his own ornithopter, a mechanism invented 500 years ago but still not completely perfected.

Volodymyr has been mesmerized by the concept of flight for his entire life. To begin with, he spent a long time studying its theory. There was no easy access to the Internet at that time, so he would search for information from any source he could - he read the Soviet magazines *Kryla Batkivshchyny* ('The Wings of the Motherland') and *Tekhnika Molodi* ('Technology for Youth'), spent hours in the library in the city of Ivano-Frankivsk, studied different types of engines and researched various sources of energy. The ornithopter is his lifetime project, and he has worked on it all by himself.

'An ornithopter is a tough nut to crack. It is harder to construct than a delta plane or a car. A car has more details, that's true, but to have at least a 10-metre flight is way more difficult. The air is an environment that is more complicated and dangerous than the earth. It will not forgive you any mistake. That's why it's more challenging.'

Alina Kondratenko

Polonyna on the Sokilskyi Crest

Spouses Vasyl and Maria Petrychuk live and work on Sokilskyi Crest, between the villages of Babyn and Yavoriv. During the grazing season, which lasts for four months, Vasyl takes his herd to the mountain meadows ('polonyna') every day. In the summer, the villagers entrust their sheep to Vasyl for grazing or milking and making cheese. The couple earn their living this way during warmer months. In the winter, the sheep give birth to their lambs. Also during the cold season, the Petrychuks look after their smallholding, and Maria makes 'lizhnyks' (blankets from sheep wool) and woollen footwear that she sells.

Cheese-making does not bring in big profits. Despite this, and their advancing years, the Petrychuks have no plans to give up breeding sheep.

'Well, we've got used to the fact that we must do it. Young people don't want to engage in this work. They want a lot of money, and there isn't much here. We are pretty old, and we are absolutely fine with the amount we get.'

Mykyta Zavilinskyi   159

A serpentine bend on the road into the town of Turka.

Lizhnyks from Yavoriv

A 'lizhnyk' is a blanket woven from sheep's wool. They were traditionally made in the Hutsul village of Yavoriv and used in ceremonies and daily life. People use them to cover beds, benches and carts; they also wrap themselves up in lizhnyks in winter.

'The thing we like about our art is its uniqueness — you won't find the same anywhere else in the world. We are simple people, but we create something that's one-of-a-kind.'

Many villagers in Yavoriv have looms at home, which is why locals become involved in lizhnyk-making from childhood. The technology is traditional - wool is spun into yarn, then a blanket is woven, then felted, then combed out.

Alina Kondratenko, Mykyta Zavilinskyi   163

The Carpathian Tram

The Carpathian tram is a narrow-gauge mountain train with a 100-year-old history. It is one of four narrow-gauge train lines with a rail width of 750 millimetres. The train route starts in the village of Vyhoda and goes through the Carpathians following the Mizunka River. It was built for timber transportation, survived two world wars and has changed ownership a couple of times. Every weekend, travellers can take a trip and enjoy a theatrical performance. The train line is a tourist attraction that boosts the development of the town's infrastructure. At the interactive narrow-gauge train museum in Vyhoda you can operate a train and watch a film about its history.

Pavlo Pashko, Dmytro Bartosh   165

Polonyna Krynta

Polonyna Krynta ('polonyna' is a Ukrainian word for a mountain meadow in the Carpathians) is famous for its tradition of Hutsul cheese-making. Today, very few people are involved in this craft. A shepherd who grazes cows at Krynta is known as a 'bovhar'. Vasyl Kirmoshchuk, from the village of Verkhovyna, is head of the bovhars and started to make cheese when he was 12 years old. Gradually he is turning grazing cattle and cheese-making into a profitable business. The cattle are gathered from smallholdings in nearby villages. As a rule, cattle owners entrust their cows only to bovhars they know personally.

Cheese is made on the polonyna itself - the average quantity in autumn is 25 kilograms, and the summer average is 50 kilograms. Salt is the only additional ingredient.

'Every country and every corner of the world make their own cheese and try to stick to this tradition. Just like we do. People understand that it's tasty, eco-friendly and without any additives.'

Alina Kondratenko, Pavlo Pashko

Christmas in Kryvorivnia

Koliada (Ukrainian traditional carol singing) in the Carpathian village of Kryvorivnia is famous for its authenticity and the number of people who take part. It lasts for the whole Christmas period. Compared to other Hutsul villages, Kryvorivnia has the largest number of Koliada singing groups or 'vatahas', which consist of people living in different districts of the village. Even the smallest district that includes just 20 houses has its own vataha.

Every vataha is led by a carol singer called 'Bereza' (which means 'birch' in Ukrainian). This is usually an older man who decides on the lyrics for each household and a routine of 'plies' (a traditional display to accompany Christmas carols). Carol singers follow the routine turning 'bartkas' - traditional Hutsul axes - in their hands.

Bukovyna

The fortress of Khotyn is one of the oldest strongholds in Ukraine. Rising above the Dnister, it used to protect the crucially important water trade route. Even though the stone walls date back to the 13th century, building continued up until the 18th century. The outpost's 40-metre-high walls have withstood multiple attacks over the years. However, military assaults would always fail unless the attackers undertook a long-lasting siege.

Today, it is a historical and architectural conservation area, used as a venue for medieval tournaments.

Malanka Celebrations in Krasnoyilsk

Malanka, a traditional holiday on the eve of St Basil's day, or New Year's Day according to the Julian calendar, is celebrated according to local traditions, mainly in villages in Bukovyna and Halychyna.

One of the most spectacular events takes place in Krasnoyilsk, a village near the border with Romania. Every year an unusual procession is watched by a large audience.

For two days, all eyes are on the carnival. Locals dress up as animals and characters from folklore. While the design of the outfits and masks may vary, the main characters remain the same.

Though the name of the carnival originates from the female character Malanka, the procession only includes men. However, girls are allowed to play the characters of Queens

and Gypsies during the main celebration, when they tour the houses of the village, accompanied by their 'Bears' on the morning of 13 January.

The Bears' costumes are made from hay or straw that would have been harvested in the summer.

Oleksandr Khomenko 175

The Pamir Radar Station

Pamir, an abandoned radar station in Bukovyna, used to be a high-security facility established on Mount Tomnatyk, not far from the Romanian border.

Five antenna domes, 1,565 metres high, are what remain of the surveillance system.

The multidirectional antennas provided continuous monitoring for about 30 years from 1960. Today, this area is surrounded by tourist trails, and is popular with travellers as an overnight stop.

Vasyl Salyha, Pavlo Pashko   177

Ionike Semeniuk's Museum in Hrushivka

Ionike Semeniuk, who is 80 years old, not only takes care of a large museum dedicated to the Moldovan villages of Hrushivka and Voloka, but also has the energy to race through the villages with his former classmate, driving his IZH-49 motorcycle, made in 1951.

The villagers cherish their Moldovan traditions and work hard to keep them alive. Voloka is famous for the large-scale production of wedding dresses. In Ionike's museum, you can find old weaver's looms that were used to make dresses some hundred years ago.

Chernivtsi, Violins by Volodymyr Solodzhuk

The sound of the violins made by Volodymyr Solodzhuk is created in a tiny workshop in Chernivtsi. His instruments touch people's hearts in concert halls all over the world. Volodymyr gave up a long career as a factory engineer in favour of the violins that had fascinated him from childhood. The craftsman, who is self-taught, later got the chance to study in Italy. In total, he has made over 200 instruments.

Volodymyr makes his violins by hand. Despite knowing everything and more about the structure and operation of musical instruments, Volodymyr does not play one himself. Volodymyr believes you can either be good at making instruments or at playing them. Wood is an exceptionally important component of high-quality violin sound. Parts of the instrument are made of different types of wood, such as spruce and maple, as each has its own unique qualities.

'Why spruce? Because it carries a sound wave faster than any other material. Why maple? Because a backplate made from a hardwood species retains a 27-kilogramme cord tension for 300 years. It must be done right, with no frills. Maple carries sound faster than any other hardwood types. These two types of wood - maple and spruce - are just what you need.'

Chernivtsi National University is based in the former Residence of Bukovynian and Dalmatian Metropolitans. The red-brick building with towers and stone carvings was built in the 19th century. It is a mix of Romanesque and Byzantine styles with Gothic, Moorish and other motifs. The architectural complex includes three buildings - a Palace, a Seminary and a Monastery.

The buildings are embellished with mouldings, carved cornices and tiles in five different colours. Chernivtsi National University is a popular sightseeing attraction and is a UNESCO World Heritage Site.

Malanka Celebrations in Vashkivtsi

On 13 and 14 January, the village of Vashkivtsi in the Bukovyna region becomes a venue for the traditional theatrical celebrations of Malanka; it is known by locals as 'Pereberia', which means 'costume party'. Since the end of the 19th century, when villagers began to dress up in costumes and masks, the Malanka celebrations in Vashkivtsi have become an amazing carnival.

Dressing in traditional costume for Malanka used to be banned by both the Romanian and Soviet governments. Nevertheless, after the Second World War, villagers still took part in celebrations, breaking Soviet laws. Up to the present day, Malanka has remained a splendid occasion, and is hugely popular with tourists.

Tavria

Birds fly over the dunes of a semi-desert in Tavria, near the Kinburn spit.

The Adzyhol Lighthouse

The Adzyhol Lighthouse in the middle of the Dnipro estuary is the tallest lighthouse in Ukraine. It was built to the design of engineer Vladimir Shukhov in 1911. Thousands of studs hold together the beams that comprise the 64-metre skeletal steel structure. This type of design not only made the building lighter, but also able to withstand the fiercest of storms. The lighthouse has survived wars and is still operational today. It offers a marvellous view of the Kinburn spit, Stanislav slopes and the village of Rybalche.

Yurii Stephanyak, Pavlo Pashko   191

The Buhai, the Ukrainian Tailed Drum

The buhai is a rare and extraordinary folk instrument. It attracted a lot of attention when ONUKA, the Ukrainian electro-folk band, has used it on stage while performing at the Eurovision Song Contest, which was held in Kyiv in 2017. Andrii Lopushynskyi started making buhais long before that. Andrii's previous experience in producing percussion instruments for historical societies paid off hugely when he made his first buhai.

The buhai is a cord and friction percussion instrument, where the sound is produced by the friction of a finger against its skin, or a bundle of horse hair fixed to its centre. The buhai is played using moistened fingers to pull the hair bundle using a sliding motion. The pitch of the sound depends on where the fingers stop.

In Ukraine, the buhai is usually played together with other instruments. Along with folk bands, carol singing groups play it to provide musical accompaniment.

'The buhai is an officially recognized Ukrainian folk instrument. However, people don't recognize it when they see it for the first time, mistaking it for an African instrument.'

Alina Kondratenko

A great white egret nesting site on the Kinburn spit. The great white egret lives separately from other birds and is very protective of members of its own species. They feed in flocks.

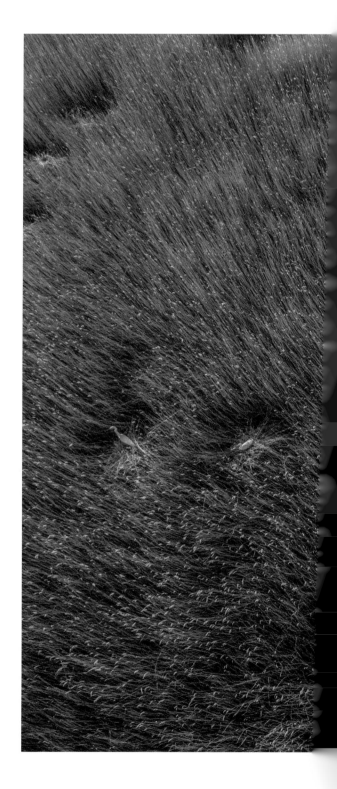

Pavlo Pashko   195

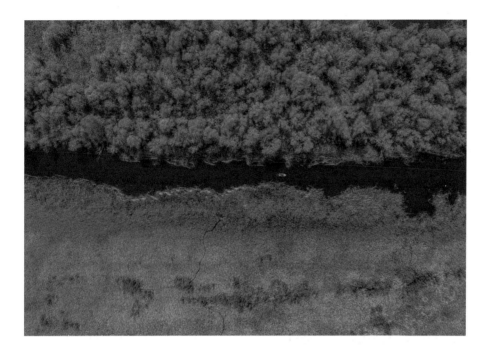

The Kherson Reed Beds

Kherson is located on the right bank of the Dnipro River, in the south of Ukraine. It became notable as the city of ships and sailors - the place where the Black Sea Navy Fleet was born. Today, it is a large sea and river port on the Dnipro. Water is an integral part of city life: it is a landmark, a place for recreation, an important resource and a source of pleasure for both children and adults. You can travel by water taxi, and in mushroom season, people sail on yachts to different sites to pick them. Larissa Shyshka, her husband and two daughters, together with coach Oleksandr Blumer, teach young sailing enthusiasts on one of the islands in Kherson.

Pavlo Pashko

Velyki Kopani and Cabbages

In the village of Velyki Kopani, near Kherson, there are hardly any households that don't grow vegetables for sale. One of the biggest wholesale vegetable markets - Nezhdanyi - is located here.

'Everyone works in the field. It's not a hobby - it's a lifestyle. It's warm here, and there is plenty of water. We are in the south. Since there is no industry here, people have no other place to work. We do our best to earn a living.'

One of the market's specialities is early-season fruits and vegetables. The prices at Nezhdanyi influence those of fruit, vegetables and berries in all parts of Ukraine since prices in Velyki Kopani provide the starting point for all the shopping centres, distributors and processing companies.

Mykyta Zavilinskyi, Pavlo Pashko   199

Stone-carved Vyshyvankas

Nova Kakhovka is a young town founded in the 1950s as a residential centre for hydroelectric complex construction workers. All the buildings here were built hastily to a standard design, and as a result are dull and featureless. Hryhorii Dovzhenko, an artist and a follower of the Boichukism style of painting (named after Mykhailo Boichuk, a Ukrainian monumentalist painter), arrived in Nova Kakhovka during that time. In collaboration with his colleagues, he created 80 unique carved panels that decorated the walls of all the buildings and changed the face of the city. The Soviet media were quick to criticize Dovzhenko for his 'architectural redundancies'. Nowadays, his creations are considered to be unique pieces of art known as 'stone-carved vyshyvankas' (traditional embroideries).

'People recall how visitors coming to Nova Kakhovka were impressed with the whitewashed houses, flourishing trees and flowers and the ornaments sparkling in the sun. The patterns on backgrounds with varying degrees of brightness and colour - violet, green, lilac - were made by artists to look like white waves. Many people said that the town looked as if it had been decorated with lace.'

Mykyta Zavilinskyi, Pavlo Pashko   201

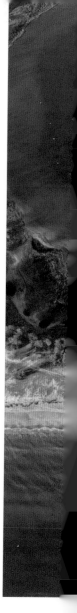

The Kinburn Spit

The Kinburn Spit separates the Dnipro-Buh estuary from the Black Sea. It is bounded by bodies of both fresh and salt water that even differ in colour. The 40-metre sand spit is an extension of the Kinburn peninsula. At its tip the sea and the estuary are just a few meters apart. It is a favourite nesting site for birds and a stopping-off point during their migration. An artificial peninsula was even created for birds next to the Lopushne lake.

Salt Lakes

Near the village of Heroiske, salt extraction is carried out in the traditional way, by gradual evaporation. The method involves moving sea water through a cascade of salt pans. Salt concentration increases by 27 per cent under the sun, and crystallization begins.

This production process has existed since 1898. However, prior to that the Cossacks (independent military units that emerged in the 15th century) used salt from this area. The ponds vary in colour depending on the concentration of beta-carotene and magnesium in the water.

Prychornomoria

The loam cliffs on the steppe shores of the Dnipro-Buh
estuary stand 40 metres high.

Olbia

Olbia is a complex of historical monuments from an ancient settlement in Prychornomoria founded as a Greek colony in the 7th century BCE. Today, it is the National Historical and Archaeological Reserve and Museum, and features artefacts from this ancient culture, including sarcophagi and various household items. The reserve includes a settlement and a necropolis. Berezan Island, where the oldest Ancient Greek settlement in Northern Prychornomoria was located, also forms part of the reserve.

With only about 17,000 visitors a year, this unique place near the city of Mykolaiv is practically an unknown destination.

Pavlo Pashko

The Bakhtov Family House

Volodymyr Bakhtov has been fascinated by the cities of ancient Greece since childhood. He fulfilled his dream to travel on a 'bireme' – a wooden ship designed to look as much like an ancient vessel as possible. This trip inspired him to move to one of these ancient cities, Olbia, where together with his wife he has built a house-workshop, to Ancient Greek design. Bakhtov's house is situated some a short distance from Olbia, in the village of Parutyne. It is not only a workshop for artists, but also a museum and gallery. Volodymyr and Tetiana reinterpret ancient Greece and create modern artworks using old techniques, visual images and even broken pieces of clay dishes that have been found in ancient Olbia.

A field in the Tylihul Nature Reserve near the village of Kobleve.

The Odesa Astronomical Observatory

Odesa Astronomical Observatory was Ukraine's main astronomical observatory during the Soviet era. It was built in 1871, and at that time there was no city or parks nearby; the conditions were perfect for observing space. However, today the lights of the coastal city of Odesa hinder normal research work here, even with all the facilities available. Instead, most observations are now carried out at the observatory's Maiaky station, 40 kilometres away.

The Aktove Canyon

The Aktove Canyon is a ravine in the steppe more than 50 metres deep formed by the River Mertvovod in the granite rocks near the village of Aktove.

Navigable up until the 20th century, the Mertvovod River is now shallow and silty. Dams constructed during the Soviet era significantly reduced water levels. The canyon is a part of the Buzkyi Hard National Nature Park.

Pavlo Pashko, Yurii Stephanyak

Sunrise at Prymorskyi Boulevard in Odesa.

Pavlo Pashko, Yurii Stephanyak

Buzkyi Hard National Nature Park

The Buzkyi Hard National Nature Park includes protected areas and geological features. With its rocky river canyons and numerous rapids, this place stands out from the steppe areas around it.

The cascade of rapids on the Southern Buh river near the village of Myhiia attracts rafting enthusiasts. The kayaking route is the second most difficult in Ukraine and is used for international rafting competitions.

A tractor ploughs a field near the modern nut farm in the village of Troitske.

Pavlo Pashko 225

Podniprovia
and Zaporizhzhia

A view of the Dnipro riverfront from
Monastyrskii Island.

Khortytsia

Khortytsia is the largest island in Dnipro, down the river from the Dnipro Hydroelectric Station in Zaporizhzhia. This is where Ukrainian history comes to life.

Khortytsia has been known for a long time because of the Dnipro rapids - rock formations in the Dnipro River between the modern cities of Dnipro and Zaporizhzhia.

However, almost a century ago, concrete dams at the Dnipro Hydroelectric Station raised the water level by 40 metres, the rapids disappeared under the water and the river became navigable.

Today, the Zaporizhian Sich historical complex, a reconstruction of a Cossack Sich (armed camp), is located on Khortytsia.

Pavlo Pashko   231

Petrykivka Painting

Petrykivka is a traditional style of painting that developed in the village of Petrykivka; however, it has spread throughout a larger area. Petrykivka painting is believed to originate from the tradition of drawing on the outside walls of village houses.

The oldest examples of the paintings, which were preserved by historians, date back to the beginning of the 20th century. In the 1930s, a school of decorative painting, where a whole generation of artisans studied, was opened in Petrykivka. This is how Petrykivka painting developed from folk art to modern art.

In 2003, Petrykivka painting was included on the Representative List of the Intangible Cultural Heritage of Humanity by UNESCO.

'Rhythm is a basis for the composition. Green leaves, blue vines, buds, flowers - all of them should be placed rhythmically. This rhythm is nothing but a reflection of life cycles, nature and space.'

Dnipro, the Potter Serhii Horban

Serhii Horban's pottery workshop is close to the city centre in Dnipro. Serhii was born in Dnipro and never formally studied pottery. He says that he learned a lot from books and the Internet. The first time he met a real potter was in the village of Opishne, in the Poltava region, which is famous for its pottery traditions. Serhii was given his first piece of clay as a gift from his friend who had already started making ceramics and used to cast wares in plaster moulds. Serhii always wanted to work with a potter's wheel – now he teaches pottery in his workshop.

Birds live on protected islands in the middle of Zaporizhzhia, near the Dnipro Hydroelectric Station and the Khortytsia National Nature Reserve.

Dobropasove, the Cucumber Centre

Dobropasove could be called a cucumber centre.
Every second household in this village has been growing
vegetables, particularly cucumbers, for generations.

Naddniprianshchyna

A rock canyon, formed from Proterozoic granite, on the Hirskyi Tikych River near the village of Buky.

Makariv, the Inventor Volodymyr Vavilov

Volodymyr Vavilov is a self-taught craftsman from the town of Makariv. He has created a fantastic car using his own hands. Volodymyr bought an old Fiat for about 150 US dollars, and since then has invested more than 10,000 US dollars renovating it. The six-wheeled car resembles a spaceship and features a model of an alien - a character from the film of the same name - that sits comfortably on the roof. This wonder-car has eight exhaust pipes, wheels with backlighting and inside there are several TVs.

'My aim was to make a car that would impress. I think I have achieved that already. I could never afford a nice car, but I can make one myself.'

The Roma of Zolotonosha

The population of Zolotonosha numbers 30,000 people, and of those 2,000 are Roma. They founded two NGOs - the Cherkasy regional NGO Romani Rota and the Zolotonosha Gypsy Commune Ame Roma. The Dialogue Between Generations Centre, which is unique in Ukraine, is a place Roma people can seek medical help, have a rest, do laundry and take a shower. The Roma of Zolotonosha are mostly engaged in trade and private entrepreneurship. There are no nomadic Roma in Zolotonosha, however there are a number of internally displaced people living in poor conditions, often without proper hygiene facilities.

Thanks to local activists, the Roma people have the opportunity to go to the same schools, churches, shops and markets as other residents. They are active participants within the city and at regional events; however, they are still not fully integrated into society.

'The aim is to integrate the Roma into Ukrainian society. I consider myself Ukrainian of Roma origin, and I'd like the others to do the same. For example, Ukrainians from Western and Eastern Ukraine are still Ukrainians. We need to build our state and our home and not be fooled by any provocations.'

Alina Kondratenko

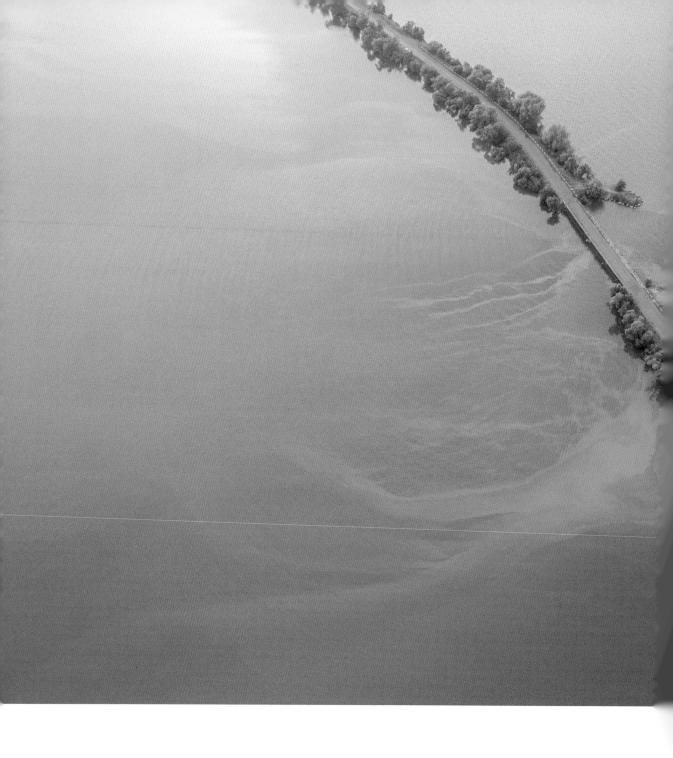

The Revivka Dam between the city of Svitlovodsk and the
village of Podorozhnie.

Goat Farms

From the beginning of the 2000s, goat farms began to emerge and develop in Ukraine. Previously, this type of farming was highly unpopular - in the Soviet Union, a goat was not considered to be a profitable animal. During our expedition to Naddniprianshchyna, we were lucky to visit four goat farms: Zolota Koza ('Golden Goat'), Babyni Kozy ('Grandma's Goats'), Lisova Ferma ('Forest Farm') and Pani Koza ('Mrs Goat'). Today there is a great deal of information on the benefits of goat's milk, so the demand for goat's-milk products in urban areas has increased.

Kateryna Akvarelna, Pavlo Pashko   251

Guitars from Bila Tserkva

Universum Guitars is a guitar factory that was founded in Bila Tserkva in 2016. To begin with prototypes were made and given to musicians to test. They were then improved according to the feedback that was received.

One of the first guitars to be designed here has both acoustic and electroacoustic modes. Designer Oleksandr Doroshenko says this represents the musical know-how of Ukrainians.

'Nobody in the world had been doing it before we did. We were the first to put a condenser microphone inside the box-frame instrument. There is a mix between the microphone and the sensor – that is what electroacoustic mode means.'

Kateryna Akvarelna   253

The Dakhovskis' Mansion

The Dakhovskis' Mansion is a previously unrecognized, unique architectural monument that was built in the village of Leskove in the 19th century. According to legend, the palace was built to outdo Count Potocki, who established Sofiivka landscape park in the town of Uman. The landowner, Dakhovskyi, decided to create a palace in the style of an English medieval castle. Built in the 1850s, the scale and scope of the palace is impressive.

During the Soviet era, the mansion was taken over by the Soviet military, and acquired the status of a regime object. Its location was kept secret.

Both in the past and today, the high architectural value of the estate was not fully appreciated. During Soviet times, the palace also served as a camp for pioneers (a youth organization in the USSR), a military hospital and a storage facility for medicines.

The estate still belongs to the Ministry of Defence of Ukraine – access is possible only with permission from a military unit commander.

Zernoland in Ivkivtsi

An open-air museum dedicated to bread-making is located in the village of Ivkivtsi. Nazar Lavrinenko, together with his team, restored an authentic mill there. Visitors to Zernoland can take part in in all stages of bread-making.

The complex has its own smithy, pottery, ethnographic museum and an area featuring table-top games played by the Haidamakas, Ukrainian paramilitary groups who fought against Polish-Lithuanian rule in the 18th century.

Volyn

This green tunnel encloses the railway between the villages of Klevan and Orzhiv. This place is especially familiar to Japanese people thanks to movie director Akiyoshi Imazeki, who featured it in his romantic drama *Tunnel of Love: The Place for Miracles,* in 2014.

The Luge Track in Kremenets

The Ukrainian Summer Luge Championship takes place at Ukraine's only wooden luge track in the town of Kremenets. It was not until the mid-1990s that the reconstruction of the 1,157-metre-long luge track began; the original track was built in the 19th century. It belongs to the sports training centre that hosts international sleigh and roller skate races every year.

The first ski-jump slopes and downhill runs built around Kremenets established it as a centre for winter sports in the 1930s. It is now used as a training base for professional athletes. However, from April to October, tourists also may go for a spin on the less challenging sections of the track.

Tarakaniv Fort

These are the remains of a unique military facility from the late 19th century. The fort is situated next to the town of Dubno, not far from the village of Tarakaniv. Oddly enough, the facility still belongs to the armed forces, even though it has been many years since it was last used for military purposes.

The fort's design is attributed to the German military engineer Eduard Totleben, who was commissioned by the Russian Empire. The fort marked the border between the Russian and Austro-Hungarian empires after the Third Partition of Poland in 1795.

The fort was built quickly between the 1870s and 1880s. New materials such as concrete, in addition to bricks and stones, were later used to make further improvements until as late as 1908.

The fort is diamond-shaped, up to 240 metres wide on each side. On the outside, it is surrounded by a deep trench and earth mounds, reinforced with thick walls. In the centre there are two-storey barracks that can be accessed through four underground passages from beneath the second earth mound.

Lubart's Castle, the Upper Castle of Lutsk, is one of two partly preserved castles and one of the oldest buildings in the region.

The Ostroh Academy

Ostroh Academy, the first ever university in Eastern Europe, was founded by Prince Kostyantyn of Ostroh in 1576. A year before, he had established a printing house here and invited Ivan Fedorovych (the founder of book printing and publishing in Ukraine) to develop it. After the prince's death, the academy fell into disrepair. The same fate befell the town of Ostroh. Under Soviet rule, the town acquired a reputation for its mental health clinic, where 'rebellious' academics and intellectuals were held.

In the early 1990s, a campaign began to revive the university in Ostroh. Ihor Pasichnyk was appointed as its principal, and he began to recruit young people who were not intimidated by the prospect of starting a university

from scratch that also needed to match the standards of universities through the world. Applicants were required to meet strict selection criteria, such as English language proficiency, a willingness to do an internship abroad, in-depth knowledge and excellent teaching skills.

'I am interested in shaping a community of Ukrainian intellectuals, young people who would not seek a better life abroad. But even if they do, I want them to work in the field matching their degree.'

A fisherman's hut in the village of Staryi Solotvyn in the middle of the Kodnianka River. Once an abandoned hut surrounded by water, it is now a small island that has become a popular tourist destination.

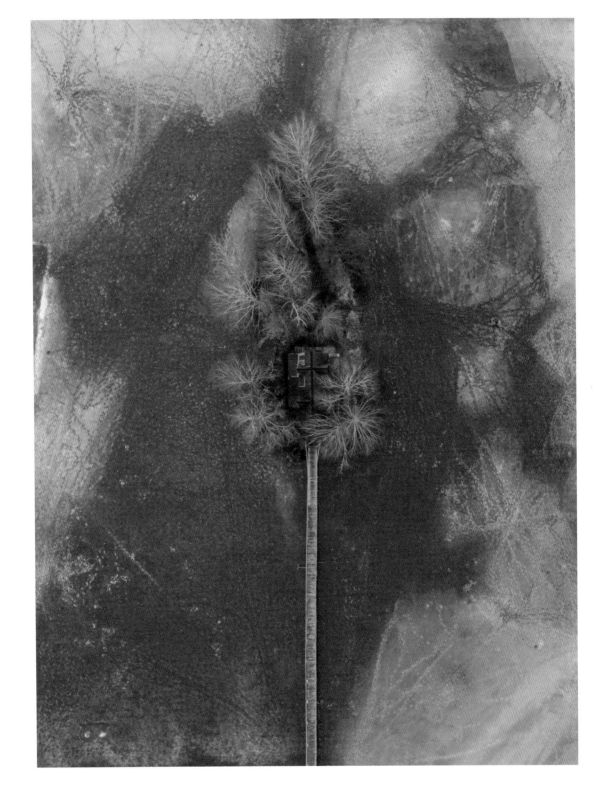

Pavlo Pashko   271

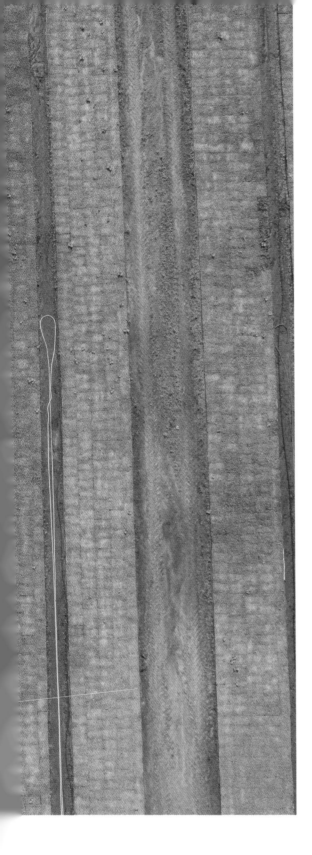

The Chinese Cabbage Centre in Khorokhoryn

Thanks to some entrepreneurs, the village of Khorokhoryn has turned into a centre for growing strawberries and Chinese cabbage. There is not a single household that is not occupied with farming or engaged in some way with the supply chain.

It all began after some villagers went to Poland for seasonal work and came back with Chinese cabbage seeds. They were following the example of the Polish farmer for whom they had been working for some years, and started to grow the same crop back at home. In those days, over half of the households were abandoned at certain times of year because their owners used to earn their living in Poland. However, as cabbage growing proved to be successful, it inspired other people to do the same. No one considers seasonal work abroad as an option these days. Cabbage and strawberries grown in Khorokhoryn are sold across Ukraine and exported to Belarus.

Slobozhanshchyna

The Slovo House

Slovo (meaning 'word' in Ukrainian), a residential building in Kharkiv, has become a symbol of the Soviet purge against intellectuals. It used to be a writers' housing cooperative, and its former residents are now regarded as the authors of the canon of Ukrainian literature. In the 1930s, most of them were persecuted and later executed. The building is still residential today.

Derzhprom, the House of State Industry

Thirteen-storey Derzhprom was the first skyscraper in the USSR. This monument, designed in the constructivist style, is situated in Svobody Square, the largest in Ukraine. The building boasts both aesthetic and functional features, and its construction was regarded as a breakthrough. Back in the days of the Ukrainian Soviet Socialist Republic, Kharkiv needed buildings like this to maintain its status as capital. Construction was stopped twice due to a lack of funding. However, five years after Derzhprom had been built in Kharkiv, Kyiv became the capital city once again.

Pavlo Pashko 279

Air Patrol

The community organization Civil Air Patrol was established in Kharkiv after the Maidan Revolution in 2014 and the Russian military assault against Ukraine. Ever since then, Civil Air Patrol has saved countless lives and provided assistance in protecting Ukrainian borders.

This is a community of qualified pilots who do their job voluntarily using private aircraft. Yurii Pokusai, the head of the organization, believes that personal efforts are enough to change the country for the better.

Besides undertaking patrols, they provide training for cadets in Kharkiv. Members of the Civil Air Patrol see themselves as successors to the pilots of the Ukrainian People's Republic, which fought against the Russian Bolshevik army, effectively fulfilling military tasks at the beginning of the 20th century.

Pavlo Pashko, Serhii Sverdelov

A view of UTR-2, the largest telescope in the world, located outside the town of Chuhuyiv in Slobozhanshchyna. It is worth noting that the area of this radio telescope is larger than the total area of all telescopes of the same type in the world.

The Meskhetian Turks

The Meskhetian Turks are a nation scattered around the world. The roots of ethnic Turks go back to the territory known today as Georgia, Meskheti in particular. The Meskhetian Turks are one of the USSR nations that were exposed to repression and expelled from the Caucasus on Stalin's order in 1944. All Meskhetian Turks were expelled from Georgia and fled to Kazakhstan, Uzbekistan and Azerbaijan.

In 1989, after the Fergan Pogroms of Uzbeks, which resulted in a hundred casualties and the burning of more than 700 homes, the Meskhetian Turks began to emigrate in search of new places to live. This is how they found themselves in Ukraine.

This photo was taken in the village of Vasiukivka, some kilometres away from demarcation line of the territory controlled by the DNR terrorist organization.

The Potters of Sloviansk

Sloviansk has been long known for its ceramic wares that are made in made in tiny pottery workshops, of which there are several hundred. For years, these workshops made souvenirs for resort towns, businesses and large companies. During the occupation of Sloviansk by the DNR terrorist organization, some workshops were ransacked and needed to be rebuilt.

For many people, this was a turning point that caused them to reconsider their target customers, and opt for Western Ukraine instead of Crimea, Donetsk and Luhansk. Potters in Sloviansk are concerned about the future of their region, which is why they donate some of their income to support the Ukrainian Army.

The Goryuns

Goryun is the name of the indigenous people of the Putyvl district, an ethnic group that originated in this area in the 16th century. Lukeriia Kosheleva, a Goryun by birth, meets a fellow villager outside her house in the village of Nova Sloboda, Slobozhanshchyna.

The dialect of the Goryun is gradually disappearing, but it can still be heard among the locals. Their language includes Ukrainian, Russian and Belorussian words. According to one theory, the name Goryun was used to designate people in mourning; while another one suggests that the name came from the fact that people settled in areas of burned forests.

Artem Halkin 289

Halychyna

Olesko Castle

Olesko Castle, the oldest castle in Halychyna, is an architectural monument from the 13th-18th centuries. The location of the castle on the border of Lithuania and Poland led to a continuous struggle for control of the place and there have been frequent changes in ownership. The first time the castle was mentioned in historical sources was in 1327.

The castle is famous in Polish history as the place where a grandson of Jan Danilowicz, the future king of Poland Jan III Sobieski, was born in 1629. During his reign, the castle was granted the status of a royal residence. During the Soviet era, it was turned into a POW camp and a military storage facility. It was only in the 1970s that renovation was able to begin.

Emmaus-Oselya

The mutual aid community Emmaus-Oselya is an NGO with a mission to help homeless people regain their dignity in the community and reintegrate into society. The community, in turn, learns to accept each person and spreads the ideas of Emmaus International, a solidarity-based movement, acting against poverty and exclusion.

Based in Lviv and supported by Emmaus International, Oselya aims to facilitate people's return to society by providing them with a manageable amount of work and with accommodation. Everyone works on a daily basis in the group's two second-hand shops and furniture workshop; any profits are equally distributed and spent on common needs. Since the organization has no external funding, it operates solely on the money it makes.

Alina Rudya   295

Domazhyr

Domazhyr is a bear shelter near Lviv. Animals that have been kept at hunting training centres, travelling zoos and circuses in horrible conditions for long periods of time receive rehabilitation in the shelter.

The rescued animals learn to live in a semi-forest environment inside spacious enclosures. Some bears experience walking on the ground for the first time, while others re-learn their natural skills. After living in captivity, bears can't return to the wild completely.

'It is great to know that we are not alone - more shelters mean more opportunities to solve the problem. Human interference in nature is destructive. The sooner people realize it, the better the chances to increase population of wild animals in natural habitat.'

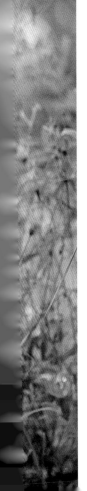

Lyres by Hordii Starukh

Lviv sculptor and musician Hordii Starukh has set himself the goal of learning to make lyres and to produce 300 of them. This is not a random number – there is evidence that in the 1930s the Soviet authorities organized a convention for musicians that played the 'kobza' (a Ukrainian folk musical instrument from the lute family), and then murdered all 300 participants. In 2009, Hordii Starukh produced his first lyre. Since then he has made dozens and has customers as far away as South Korea.

He is self-taught and continues to work on his technique and the instruments to make them sound exceptional. Hordii makes the keys and the sounding boards by hand. He attaches his distinctive handle, which is spiral-shaped, unlike the traditional European S-shaped ones. Each lyre is one of a kind and has a unique sound.

During the years of the Soviet regime, the craft of lyre-making declined, but Hordii is now re-establishing it. He says that even though he relies on traditions, he makes modern instruments.

'I have a dream to make at least 300 lyres. The history surrounding this art, with the execution of our bards, is a sad one. I will never be able to completely restore the craft of lyre manufacturing, but I will at least do what I can to contribute to its revival and continue it. If I manage to make 300 lyres, my mission will be complete.'

!FESTrepublic

One of the most famous regenerated industrial environments in Lviv is !FESTrepublic, which provides offices, modern workshops and free zones for visitors. It was created by Lviv Holding of Emotions !FEST, founded by entrepreneurs Andrii Khudo, Yurii Nazaruk and Dmytro Herasimov in 2007. In 2015, they purchased an abandoned factory premises Halychsklo ('Halychyna Glass') located in the industrial district of Pidzamche.

The factory used to produce glass vessels for the pharmaceutical industry but following bankruptcy it remained vacant for about 10 years. In the autumn of 2016, !FESTrepublic Club, a venue for discos and parties, opened at the premises. In the summer of 2018, !FEST Coffee Mission Hub also opened its doors.

In 2010, Lviv Holding of Emotions !FEST became partners with the publishing house Vydavnytstvo Staroho Leva ('Old Lion Publishing House'). The headquarters of the publishing house is located on the site of the !FESTrepublic in a building that looks like a huge bookshelf.

Alina Rudya, Pavlo Pashko

Vytynankas by Dariia Alyoshkina

Vytynanka (the art of paper-cutting) appeared around Ukraine as a means of decorating rural houses from the middle of the 19th century. The art of vytynanka was considered lost for a while, though a woman from Lviv has discovered a new way of attracting attention to this Ukrainian craft by creating vytynankas for modern interiors, public places and book covers. Dariia creates large-scale vytynanka curtains that have already found customers in Poland, France and even South Korea.

'I started making large-format vytynankas and managed to draw attention to them by creating a "wow" effect. Later on, people started learning what vytynanka is about and that the tradition still exists because vytynanka art was considered lost back in 2008.'

Sunset on Parashka Mountain

Sunset on Parashka (Paraska) mountain, the highest peak of the range in the Skole Beskydy National Nature Park in the Carpathians. The mountain is 1,268.5 metres above sea level.

The Swiss Farm in Potutory

In 2007, a Swiss woman, Cristina Lieberherr, arrived to live and work in the village of Potutory, near Berezhany. She organized an enterprise that grows ecologically clean tea and herbs.

Cristina came to Ukraine to represent an investor from an organization that encourages small farmers to implement organic farming methods. She had some experience and recipes for creating herbal mixes that she decided to use for her own venture. During the first year, Cristina did everything herself, but today she has several full-time employees.

They grow Ukrainian dill at the farm, which is regarded as a rare and valuable plant in Switzerland. They also grow sage, chamomile, mint and giant hyssop. Volunteers and tourists are welcome at the farm.

'Everyone who visits Berezhany area admires our hills and forests. During the Austro-Hungarian Empire, this area was called 'little Switzerland'. The Swiss came here, fell in love with the place, and decided to implement a project aimed at the development and support of biodynamic agricultural management in Ukraine.'

The Skarbova Hora Ranch

In the village of Lopushna near Lviv, Ostap Lun has founded a ranch called Skarbova Hora ('Treasure Mountain'). His love for horses inspired him to start a socially beneficial community, including a hynotherapy centre, which has operated since 2010.

Ever since childhood, Ostap had dreamed about horse riding, but he managed to make this a reality as an adult. He owns a garment-manufacturing business in Lviv that

gives him the opportunity and resources to maintain the ranch.

'I am happy with my lifestyle. Everything here is real. I simply notice this power of nature that is delicate and strong at the same time.'

Interaction with horses has physical and emotional benefits. Hynotherapy has a positive effect on children

with disabilities. A horse has to be trained every day for four years so that it is able to work with children.

Ostap has developed a special way to communicate with horses. It comprises mainly of body language because horses react mostly to gestures and body posture.

Kateryna Akvarelna, Khrystyna Kulakovska

The Doors to be Preserved

'Frankivsk that has to be preserved' is the name of a civil movement in Ivano-Frankivsk that was established with the aim of preserving its heritage. It was founded by activist Mariia Kozakevych in 2016 in order to maintain the old entrance doors of historic buildings in Ivano-Frankivsk.

Over a couple of years, the movement succeeded in assembling a team of carpenters, blacksmiths and stained-glass designers who are involved with restoration, as well as activists who raise awareness. In just a short time they have managed to save about 20 doors that were found on rubbish tips and returned them to their original locations instead of replacing them with new plastic doors.

'The name of our organization reflects the state of things in the city - it really needs to be cared for.'

Ivano-Frankivsk is a relatively young city and still carries memories of its founders - the Potocki family - as well as recollections of the Austro-Hungarian and West Ukrainian People's Republic periods. Every era left some mark on the city: exquisitely embellished mansions, the foundations of Bastion (the fortress of Stanislav, the former name of Ivano-Frankivsk, from the 17th-19th centuries), churches and residential houses. The doors and windows were made out of high-quality timber due to the city's proximity to the forests of Carpathia.

Khrystyna Kulakovska   311

Questions and Answers

Why is the project called Ukraïner?

The title came about as a result of combining two words expressing the main idea of the project: 'Ukraine' and 'insider', as we show Ukraine to both Ukrainians and the world from the position of an insider.

How do we divide Ukraine by regions?

The book has 16 chapters. Each chapter covers one historical region of Ukraine, based on the historical and ethnographic borders at the beginning of the 20th century. After the Second World War, the current regional borders were established, which allowed the Soviet authorities to wield their power more efficiently. Our aim is to unify the country, so therefore here we use historical regions instead of those established by the Soviet Union.

Why do we write toponyms in this way?

The League of Nations, the United Nations and other international organizations began the process of the unification of toponyms, transliterating them in accordance with the single international standard, in the 20th century. During the process of the transliteration standards development, Ukraine was part of the Soviet Union, and therefore had no say within the international arena. All international documents concerning the Soviet Ukraine used toponyms transliterated from the Russian language - the official language of the Soviet Union - despite their Ukrainian origin. The results of this transliteration policy can be seen in Ukraine and the world even today. A prime example is that Ukraine's capital is still referred to as 'Kiev' (transliteration from Russian) instead of 'Kyiv' (transliteration from Ukrainian). In this book and in all the other materials of Ukraïner, we use a transliteration of Ukrainian toponyms from the Ukrainian language, in order to rectify the situation.

About Ukraïner

Ukraïner originated as a small volunteer community of enthusiastic individuals, united by a common desire to explore and document Ukraine, and to showcase it both to fellow Ukrainians and the wider world. Since 2016, the team has been making expeditions to all of the country's historical regions. We collect people's stories and film terabytes and terabytes of photo and video material. Today, Ukraïner is no longer just a community of like-minded people, but an organization with more than 700 volunteers who work together as professional teams. These teams are busy producing, researching, conducting interviews, filming, taking photographs, transcribing and subtitling videos, writing and editing texts, translating and presenting our content to the global community.

A significant portion of Ukraïner's multimedia materials are stories of success, change, reform, the preservation of heritage and historical memory, as well as explainers about the essence of who we are: our language, history, culture, and more. We are also constantly looking for new formats to broadcast our content within our country and abroad, and we translate our materials into other languages for videos, social media, films, podcasts, and books.

For a long time, the Ukrainian context was forced to take a back seat, suppressed by Russian imperialism not just throughout the world, but also in Ukraine itself. Each successive generation of Ukrainians grew increasingly distanced from an awareness of their identity and the value of their land, culture, customs and shared past. This is why Ukraïner started telling stories from all over Ukraine, helping people to understand the value of our country.

On 24 February 2022, Russia launched a full-scale war against Ukraine.

On the same day, Ukraïner relaunched all its communication channels and started broadcasting about the war and the way Ukraine is overcoming the disasters brought upon it by the occupying forces. Stories about the resilience of the Ukrainian people – told in different languages, on various platforms – became one of the most vital priorities.

Since the start of the full-scale war, Ukraïner has been collecting the stories of evacuees, documenting initiatives that provide humanitarian and military support, recording interviews with activists and debunking Russian propaganda. At the same time, we are still publishing books about contemporary and living Ukrainian history, as well as collections of photos that continue to represent our country.

Ukraïner remains a global platform of stories from Ukraine. Yet, if previously those stories portrayed a peaceful country changing and reforming, today they are about a country fighting for its freedom, with reports of fierce struggles, resilience, heroism and dedication to the cause. Today, Ukrainians are sharing their experience of courageous resistance and victories with the whole world, and explaining why the world needs to fight on Ukraine's side for global democratic values.

Support Ukraïner

How to pronounce the names of regions and why these names are used.

Zakarpattia [zɐkɐrˈpatʲːɐ]
Commonly used name – Transcarpathia.
Western region separated from the rest of the territory of the country by the Carpathian mountains, situated behind (Ukrainian: за, 'za') these mountains – The Carpathians.

Pryazovia [prɪɑˈzɔːwʲɐ]
Commonly used name – The Azov Sea Region.
Region next to the Azov sea in the south, meaning situated by (Ukrainian: при, 'pry') the Azov sea.

Poltavshchyna [pʊˈltɑːʏ ʃtʃɪnɐ]
Commonly used name – The Poltava Region.
Region on the left bank of the Dnipro River, between the Naddniprianshchyna to the West and the Slobozhanshchyna to the East. The name of the region derives from the name of the river Ltava.

Polissia [pʊˈlisʲːɐ]
Region in the north-west of the country, covered with forests, as if hidden behind (Ukrainian: по, 'po') the forest (Ukrainian: ліс, 'lis').

Bessarabia [bɪsːɐˈrɑːbʲɐ]
Region in the south-west, situated between the Prut and the Dnister rivers, the mouth of the Danube river and the Black sea. It is also called Budzhak (Turkish: 'Bucak' – 'corner'). This region was named by Osman (Turkish) conquerors centuries ago, from the way it was situated.

Sivershchyna [ˈsʲiːʏ ɪrʃtʃɪnɐ]
Region in the north, the name of which derives from the Siveriany tribe, who populated the area during the period of the Kyivan Rus.

Podillia [pʊˈdʲiːlʲɐ]
Region situated in the valley of the Pivdennyi Buh and the Dnister rivers, as if at the bottom ('podil' – bottom of something).

The Carpathians [kɑːrˈpeɪθjənz]
Commonly used name – The Carpathian Mountains.
Mountain region and the west of Ukraine. Covers Lemkivshchyna, Boikivshchyna and Hutsulshchyna, the regions of mountain ethnic groups of Ukrainians.

Bukovyna [bʊkʊˈʏɪnɐ]
Region in the west, the name of which derives from the Slavic word 'buk' (Ukrainian: бук – beech) and means 'beech forest' or 'beech land'.

Tavria [ˈtɑwrʲɐ]

Region in the south, next to the Black sea; covers the southern part of mainland Ukraine and the Crimean peninsula. The name of the region derives from the ancient tribe of Tavrs that lived here.

Prychornomoria [prɪˌtʃɔrnoˈmɔːrʲɐ]

Commonly used name – The Black Sea Region.

Region is situated by (Ukrainian: при, 'pry') the Black sea, along its northern coast.

Naddniprianshchyna [nɐḍ ːnʲɪˈprʲɑnʲʃtʃɪnɐ]

Commonly used name – Dnieper Ukraine.

Central region, situated in the upper valley, as if over (Ukrainian: над, 'nad') the Dnipro river.

Podniprovia and Zaporizhzhia [poḍ ːnʲɪˈprɔːwʲɐ] [zɐpoˈrʲiʒʲːɐ]

Commonly used name – The Dnipro and Zaporizhzhia Steppes.

Steppe region, situated behind the rapids (Ukrainian: 'porohy') of the Dnipro river.

Volyn [woˈlɪnʲ]

Region in the north-west, the name of which derives from the name of the ancient city of Volyn.

Slobozhanshchyna [sloboˈʒɑːnʲʃtʃɪnɐ]

Commonly used name – Sloboda Ukraine.

Region named after a type of settlement, 'sloboda' – a big village or town – which were spread across the region many years ago.

Halychyna [ɦɑlɪtʃɪˈnɑː]

Commonly used name – Galicia.

Region in the west, the name of which derives from the ancient city of Halych, once the capital of the Kingdom of Galicia.

Volunteers, who took part in the project between June 2016 and July 2019:

Aleksandr Maiorov

Aleksandr Sirota

Aleksey Sobchuk

Alexander Legostaev

Alexandra Baklanova

Alexey Panchenko

Alina Kobernik

Alina Kondratenko

Alina Rudya

Alisa Smyrna

Alla Mandziuk

Alona Kabaliuk

Anastasia Koberska

Anastasiia Baklytska

Anastasiia Yakubyshyn

Anastasiya Blazhko

Andrew Sacheva

Andrii Bozhok

Andrii Illin

Andrii Kuzminskyi

Andrii Rohozin

Andrii Sydoruk

Andrii Zavertanyi

Andriy Bocharov

Ania Yabluchna

Anka Yemelyanova

Ann Ivanova

Anna Kubareva

Anna Chapala

Anna Dragula

Anna Holban

Anna Kondratyuk

Anna Lukasevych

Anna Maniati

Anna Vorobiova

Anna Yemelianova

Anton Protsiuk

Anton Shynkarenko

Anton Veklenko

Artem Halkin

Artem Rusko

Artem Zubkevych

Bogdan Logvynenko

Bogdan Suiunbaiev

Bogdana Korogod

Bohdan Lopatiy

Bohdanna Kapitsa

Bohdanna Korohod

Britta Ellwanger

Claire Little

Daniel Mecineanu

Daria Salo

Daria Temerbek

Daryna Ariamnova

Daryna Kyrychok

Dasha Pyrogova

Denys Antonchyk

Denys Bloshchynskyi

Diana Butsko

Diana Dalkevych

Diana Horban

Diana Staretska

Dmitriy Bartosh

Dmytro Bezverbnyi

Dmytro Chernenko

Dmytro Kosheliuk

Dmytro Koshevyi

Dmytro Okhrimenko

Dorina Gakman

Elina Foinska

Evgen Madenov

Francesco Pagano

Gayana Mkrtchyan

Halya Kohuch

Halyna Kurdiukova

Hanna Ostroverkha

Hanna Tymets

Hari Krisshnan

Helen Ivashenko

Iaroslava Kravchenko

Ihor Bukalo

Illia Suprun

Ilona Badenko

Ilona Mykolaishyn

Inna Parfeniuk

Inna Sakhno

Ira Stepanova

Ira Zhukevych

Iren Nosova

Iryna Burtyk

Iryna Hlushkevych

Iryna Oparina

Iryna Pelts

Iryna Shvets

Iryna Voloshyna

Iulia Fedorovych

Iuliia Rublevska

Ivan Shegda

Ivanna Zarytska

Jurii Stephanyak

Justyna Blaszczak

Kaitlin Vitt

Karina Piliugina

Karyna Mykytiuk

Kateryna Dashko

Kateryna Kapra

Kateryna Kulykova

Kateryna Lehka

Kateryna Senchenko

Kateryna Smuk

Katya Akvarelna

Katya Keretsman

Khrystyna Arkhytka

Khrystyna Bunii

Khrystyna Kulakovska

Khrystyna Oryshchak

Khrystyna Tynkalyuk

Kira Vereshchagina

Kostia Balytskyi

Ksenia Stetsenko

Kseniia Bundziak

Ksenya Riznyk

Lasha Avkopashvili

Lesia Diak

Lesya Homyak

Lesyk Yakymchuk

Liliya Yurkiv

Lina Golovnya

Lisa Litvinenko

Liuda Kravchenko

Liza Koshevaia

Lyuda Kucher

Maddalena Mongera

Maks Kenig

Maksym Sytnikov

Malanka Junko

Maria Babchuk

Maria Fomenko

Maria Kolesnik

Maria Kovalchuk

Maria Petrenko

Maria Prokhorenko

Maria Terebus

Mariana Kizlyk

Marichka Kurylo-Aleksevych

Marichka Pohorilko

Marichka Ruban

Mariia Hlukh

Mariia Shchur

Mariia Zaichenko

Marina Fudashkina

Mariya Maksimenkova

Marta Burdiak

Marta Hrechyn

Marta Shrubkovska

Maryan Manko

Maryna Odnorog

Maryna Plutenko

Maryna Riabykina

Maryna Sarazhyn

Mateusz Baj

Max Zavalya

Michael Chumak

Mikhail Tsitou

Misha Shelest

Mykhailo Slobodian

Mykola Korol

Mykola Nosok

Myroslava Oliinyk

Nadija Kuryliak

Nadiya Krutynska

Natalia Kucheriava

Natalia Hryniuk

Natalia Kiryakova

Natalia Lysak

Natalia Panchenko

Natalia Petrynska

Natalia Stec

Natalia Vyshynska

Natalia Zinevych

Natálie Dubanevicová

Nataliia Bortnik

Nataliia Serediuk

Natalka Kursyk

Natasha Ponedilok

Nazar Matvieichev

Nazar Omelyanovych

Ndiya Rychok

Nick Zavilinskyi

Nika Kreidenkova

Oksana Krasovska

Oksana Kuzema

Oleg Sologub

Oleg Marchuk

Oleg Pereverzev

Oleksandr Bielov

Oleksandr Horobets

Oleksandr Kabanov

Oleksandr Khomenko

Oleksandr Popko

Oleksandr Portian

Oleksandr Ratushnyak

Oleksandr Rybii

Oleksandr Sloboda

Oleksandr Tartachnyi

Oleksandr Yudin

Oleksandra Kosior

Oleksandra Kyryanova

Oleksandra Vlasiuk

Oleksii Karpovych

Oleksii Yudin

Oleksiy Obolensky

Olena Vavshko

Olena Logvynenko

Olena Yermolenko

Olesia Yedynak-Khoma

Olexandra Tesliuk

Olga Gavrylyuk

Olga Kovalova

Olga Nova

Olga Teslenko

Olga tsvetkova

Olha Dmytruk

Olha Glady

Olha Honzajk

Olha Khanas

Olha Kovalchuk

Olha Reshetnyk

Olha Salimonovych

Olha Shcherbak

Olha Shevchenko

Olha Stonozhenko

Olha Stulii

Olia Chernyk

Olia Diatel

Olia Zaverach

Ollie Shor

Olya Tsuprykova

Olya Zaverach

Ondrej Cerný

Orest Rybii

Paul Danyliv

Pavlik Mudryi

Pavlo Haidai

Pavlo Pakhomeko

Pavlo Pashko

Pjotr Hiebert

Polina Zabizhko

Polina Zymina

Polya Bondaruk

Pylyp Dotsenko

Roman Hladkyh

Roman Lypak

Ruslan Veselui

Sashko Sivchenko

Sergey Korovayny

Sergii Guzenkov

Sergii Rodionov

Sergiy Kucherenko

Sergiy Polezhaka

Serhii Horbatiuk

Serhii Husakov

Serhii Nemyrovskyi

Serhii Sverdielov

Sofia Anzheliuk

Sofia Bazko

Sofia Kalash

Sofia Serhiichuk

Solomia Granger Chabursky

Solomia Husak

Solomia Vonsul

Stanislav Bielyi

Stanislav Blanco

Svitlana Borshch

Svitlana Urum

Tania Kostyuk

Tania Tarasova

Tanya Rodionova

Taras Kovalchuk

Tetiana Khuk

Tetiana Okopna

Tetiana Pasichnyk

Trayan Muse

Trayan Mustyatse

Tymur Pliushch

Vadim Syrovoj

Vadym Kruk

Valentyn Kuzan

Valentyn Pugachov

Valeriya Didenko

Varvara Verbytska

Vasyl Goshovsky

Vasyl Salyha

Vasylyna Haran

Vctoria Solodka

Victor Artemenko

Victoria Redia

Victoria Sorochuk

Vika Volyanska

Viktor Kozak

Viktoria Sypukhina

Viktoriia Savitska

Vira Brezhneva

Vitaliy Zhylak

Vlad Tsovma

Yana Bilynets

Yana Bogdanova

Yana Konyk

Yaroslav Azhnyuk

Yaroslav Karpenko

Yelizaveta Koshevaya

Yevgeniia Haydamaka

Yevgeniia Sapozhnykova

Yevhen Hlibovytsky

Ylyzaveta Chernova

Yu Kostenko

Yulia Kabanets

Yulia Plysiuk

Yulian Khorunzhyi

Yuliia Kostrovska

Yuliia Balka

Yuliia Derevianchuk

Yuliia Dyminska

Yuliia Kochetova-Nabozhniak

Yuliia Teleshova

Yuliia Turbovets

Yura Palyvoda

Yurii Pyrch